Journey through Winter

A THREE-MONTH DEVOTIONAL JOURNEY

Printed in Canada
Designed by Dean Pickup
Edited by Alicia Hein and Elaine Phillips
Printed by PageMaster Publishing

TABLE OF CONTENTS

PREFACE

In order for you, the reader, to understand this book and our journey of writing a little better, I invite you to read a letter that I wrote to our writers on the day this book was started. It was an ordinary day, except for one little phrase I heard whispered to my heart: "Now is the time." I went to my computer and wrote out a list of women I knew. Then I got on Facebook and sent a letter to each of them. This is a part of that letter.

In the last eight years, I have had a couple of extremely rough years with a lot of loss and pain and struggles. One thing that I have often craved during these times is talking with someone who has gone before me and has made it through alive! Someone who has been there and I could glean advice and wisdom from.

When I was going through one of my darkest seasons, I looked for things to read about spiritual pain and struggles and found there really isn't much out there. There were some theoretical studies on pain and suffering, but not a lot of testimony-based, practical, biblical learnings.

A couple of months ago, I was out talking with a friend of mine who has also been struggling with life and I was able to verbalize to her that 'something' that had been knocking around in my head for a while…

What I said went something like this…

"When I look at some of the women God has put in my life, it amazes me! Many of my friends have gone through deep pain—*incredible* women who have come out the other side, not bitter and resentful, but more godly and wise because of it. I would love to put all their stories and the spiritual truths they have learned through their struggles and wounds into a book as a source of wisdom as I walk through this stuff."

She said, "I'd buy that book!"

I said, "You wouldn't need to… You'd be one of them!"

That was the beginning of me thinking through the process of doing exactly that. I would like to write—and help some of the wonderful godly women I know to write—a series of seasonal devotional books to help others struggling with pain that happens through life and the trials of living in a broken world.

I have been praying for a while and your name is one I believe the Lord has laid on my heart to ask if you would like to be involved in this process.

I would like for this to not just be a clinical process of writing, but of developing a safe community of godly women that can be of encouragement to one another. My dream is that, through this community, God would use us to encourage one another, and that this would be an experience that would bring healing and great joy to you (and eventually to our readers).

I know that none of us are professional writers. I don't expect you to be. I'm asking you to be part of this because of your story and because of your heart and faith in Jesus, not because of your professional abilities as an author. I would like us to learn and grow into effective storytellers and teachers and writers together.

I can't tell you how excited I am to see what God decides to do through this!

I wrote out this letter, and hit send. Then I started praying desperately that God would have those women respond whom He wanted to be part of this book. He did. They did.

When I look back at what I initially sent out to the ladies who are now the authors of this book, it brings tears to my eyes. Tears of gratitude and joy. Tears of conviction and celebration.

This has not been an easy road! In the midst of writing *Journey Through Winter*, we walked down paths that included the loss of loved ones through cancer and accidents. We dealt with drug and alcohol abuse, arrests, abortion, illness, rape, miscarriage, self-harm, and fights with suicide and depression. We battled with all sorts of sin and broken-ness that rushed in waves through the lives of the ones we hold dearest.

But we have also seen God ... *Oh,* how we have seen God!

We bear witness to His love, mercy and tender kindness. We have seen His redemption and renewal, His grace and forgiveness. We have seen prodigals return home and watched Jesus *run* to meet them. We are walking paths of healing and forgiveness, restoration and reconcil-iation. We are on journeys of finding God in the midst of being torn apart and bound up.

Our prayer is that, as we communicate pieces of our stories on the pages of this book, you will hear and see our hearts, which are so full of thankfulness to the God of every season. We pray that you will be encouraged and fortified to walk into the seasons that come your way, and that you will know the love of the Father who walks with you in them all.

LYNDA BLAZINA lives in Cochrane, Alberta, with her husband Max. She has three adult children. Involvement in the local church has always been a huge part of her life.

Along with Max, she currently leads the Group Life portion of their church's adult ministries. She is the founder and Ministry Director for Walk With Me Ministries, and was a contributing author in *Carried: 10 Stories of Finding Supernatural Peace in the Midst of Pain and Confusion*.

After going through a couple of seasons of extreme loss and trials, she works to incorporate the things she has learned into ministering to others in pain. God's faithfulness, love and compassion are forefront whether writing, mentoring leaders or speaking.

Lynda has a heart for hearing and having women's stories heard, believing that God has given us each a story to reveal Himself and His character. Our stories are full of redemption and the love of the Father, even in our darkest moments. This belief was the driving force behind compiling *Journey Through Winter* and was the beginning of Walk With Me Ministries.

Lynda also loves to hang out with friends, putter in her yard, have a nice supper out, gather art supplies for a creative project and play board games.

To find out more about Walk With Me Ministries or to contact Lynda to have her speak at your event, you can go to wwmm.ca.

RYSHON BLAZINA lives in Cochrane, Alberta. She is currently in legal studies and unsurprisingly, loves the "letter of the law."

Ryshon has been involved in leadership and ministry ever since she was a young girl, when she talked to church leadership, then implemented and led Mini Ministries at age eight in the church plant that her family was involved in. God has been placing her in ministries that she leads with the same zest and love for the Lord to this day.

She has been involved in church planting and has been a vital part of launch teams in three churches in the past ten years. Her heart is full when she sees churches start and then thrive through people coming into relationship with Jesus.

With her outgoing, extremely extraverted personality, she thrives in community with friends. She also loves fashion and when she is able to combine fashion, trends and friends, she is in her element.

Ryshon packs a lot into each day and keeps her schedule full, so implements a time budget to keep her focused and on task. Her closest friends, although mocking her slightly for her passion for organization, wouldn't deny that she accomplishes a *lot* in a week!

Ryshon has spoken at conferences as a breakout session speaker and has preached in her church. If you are interested in booking Ryshon for a speaking engagement, you can contact her through Walk With Me Ministries at wwmm.ca.

STEFANIE CARLSON resides in Edmonton, Alberta, with her husband Drew and two daughters Lyric and Selah.

She studied cosmetology and has continued on to a successful career in the industry. After the birth of her first daughter, Stefanie opened her own hair studio and has successfully grown the business over the past seven years.

Engaging in the belief of whole-souled beauty, Stefanie embraces the importance of living in the present which is made possible by employing a balance of attending to both inner and outer wellness. Stefanie is an overcomer of sexual abuse as a young teen, and is able to use her experiences to coach and relate to many different people in several different walks of life.

As a result of her trauma, and belief in how therapy can heal, Stefanie is passionate about sharing her stories, knowing the power her words carry and how they can help encourage the healing process. She has jumped at every opportunity to write down her experiences, and was a contributing author in *Carried: 10 Stories of Finding Supernatural Peace in the Midst of Pain and Confusion* with her chapter "God Was Everywhere" in 2017.

Passionate about inner healing, healthy living and a healthy mind, Stefanie is excited to also be partnering alongside her husband Drew in an effort to bring awareness and ultimately an end to human trafficking. Stefanie shows her generosity through acts of service and quality time spent with family, friends and clients. She loves deeply, she laughs often, and she is in love with the world around her.

DEBORAH CARPENTER (HAUGAN) was born in Grande Prairie, Alberta, to Leroy and Shirley Haugan in 1971. She became a big sister to her little brother, Darcy, in 1975. Raised in Peace River, Alberta, she spent two weeks every summer at the Haugan homestead in Fosston, Saskatchewan, playing with cousins and cattle and swinging from ropes in the hayloft. Other times of the year, she took numerous Greyhound bus trips to Grande Prairie to spend time with her Gramma VanNatter and take swimming lessons at the RecPlex.

She graduated high school from Prairie Christian Academy in 1989 and followed up with college certificates in Office and Business Administration. She is currently enrolled at Briercrest College and Seminary and is working towards her Certificate of the Seminary in Biblical Theology.

If you ask her what she likes to do for fun, she will tell you that it must be an activity that allows her to drink her coffee without spilling.

She is an amazing wife to Andrew; a devoted mom to Rebekkah, Sarah, Joshua, Caleb and Grace; a grateful mother-in-law to Joshua, Cole and Sonia; and a proud grandmother to Eve, Eli and Lucas.

You can find her on Facebook and Twitter (@DebbieJayneC) and via the Walk With Me Ministries webpage (wwmm.ca). She is available for speaking engagements or a quiet conversation over a large Americano.

LISA CLARKE lives in Edmonton, Alberta, with her husband and two of her three daughters.

She joined this writing project in part to grapple with her own painful journey through tragedy. She desires her contributions to be authentic to her encounters with grief in the loss of her daughter. She desires a life of faith that faces hard truth without being flippant or preachy.

Her educational background includes studies in early childhood education, women's studies, and home economics. Her topical interests include grief recovery, conflict resolution and personal mentoring related to wellness issues.

She is a mother of three girls, two with her, entering adulthood and university and one who has passed on. She balances a life teaching preschool students, and also shares mentoring and hospitality as a university chaplain with her partner of 26 years, Bryan.

She has a heart for wellness with vulnerable and hurting students in a fast-paced and stressful system. When she isn't serving others in love, she enjoys expanding her cooking skills, wine tasting, and Pilates.

If you would be interested in Lisa sharing more of her story at your event, she can be reached at lisaannclarke@gmail.com.

BRENDA GOUDY lives in Calgary, Alberta, just a few minutes away from the beautiful Rocky Mountains. Her home should have a revolving door to accommodate her three adult boys who sometimes live away, but are always welcomed home with open arms and fresh baked cookies.

She works as an Educational Assistant at a private Christian school and loves the joys and challenges it provides. Having been at the same school for many years, she enjoys the relationships that have been made and maintained over time. She has spent many hours mentoring young people whose lives have crossed her path and believes in longevity in relationships and making connections that encourage others in their faith and identity in Christ.

This is the result of bearing many hardships in her own life. As a young woman, she did not understand or embrace her identity in Christ and made many decisions out of fear that had lasting consequences. Having survived numerous challenges over the years, Brenda came to acknowledge her worth in God's eyes and live accordingly. Her positive personality and refusal to give in to despair inspired a passion to live in freedom and hope.

Brenda is passionate about sharing God's love with others. She is often found mentoring the younger generation and sharing her experiences in order to help them make wiser choices. She loves to connect with friends over coffee or a good meal and share in life's journey with them.

She is excited to be a part of Walk With Me Ministries and share her story in *Journey Through Winter*. She can be contacted for speaking engagements through the Walk With Me website, wwmm.ca.

CONNIE LUCILLE PEACHEY is the wife of one man, the mother of three children, a mother-in-law, and a grandmother of three fabulous boys. They don't often have the opportunity to all be together under the same roof but when they do, it is bursting with noise, joy, laughter, teasing, music and feasting. It is a riot!

Connie married her soul mate, Tom Peachey, in 1985. They have partnered in pastoral ministry for over thirty years, shepherding congregations ranging in size from 45 to 245, spanning all four western provinces from tiny prairie towns to the Greater Vancouver area. Her greatest joy is working with people who long for a closer relationship with Jesus.

Tom and Connie enjoy exploring the great outdoors together in their canoe or on their mountain bikes, hiking urban and mountain trails alike. They find shalom when sitting by the campfire in their campsite.

Connie is on a journey of increasing intimacy with Jesus which began when she was four years old. He has carried her through deep waters and continues to "make a way where there seems to be no way." Recently, she celebrated her 'Year of Jubilee': 50 years of walking with Jesus! This past year, Connie contributed to *Carried: 10 Stories of Finding Supernatural Peace in the Midst of Pain and Confusion.*

Connie has spoken at women's retreats and has prepared breakout sessions for conferences. If you are interested in having Connie speak at your event, you can connect with her through wwmm.ca.

CHARLEEN RASCHKE and her husband John live in Edmonton, Alberta. She manages her adult son's program for his special needs and he lives with them full-time. They have two more adult children who live in the area with their families and three grandchildren to date.

Charleen's first published work was her memoir, *A Season of Ashes*. Since the release of her book, she has co-authored *Christmas: Stories & More* and *Carried*. She has also written articles published in FellowScript magazine.

She is involved in her local church as one of several leaders of women's ministries. She has been involved with Walk With Me Ministries since its conception in 2015. Her role with WWMM is Writing Director.

She loves to go for coffee with friends and with women in need of encouragement. In the spring till fall season, she can be found puttering around in her flower gardens. In the colder weather, she is either writing, coordinating the next renovation project or planning a trip to a warmer climate.

She has worked with youth groups in the past, mentored several younger women, taken leadership roles on mission trips and served with her husband as a mission builder for a few months.

Charleen is accepting speaking engagements and can be contacted and/or followed on her author page on Facebook (Charleen Raschke–Author); on Instagram(@charleenraschke); on her website: www.charleenraschke.ca or www.wwmm.ca or email at charleenraschke@gmail.com.

KERRY ROBIDEAU is a prayer warrior and has a heart to see women experience spiritual and emotional healing, living in the fullness of God's love and identity. She has an authentic heart and writes out of a journey of faith that has experienced a fair share of highs and lows.

She and her husband were actively involved in pastoral ministry for 13 years and it was through that she discovered a passion to see women grow in their own unique calling. Having led several small groups, Bible studies and one-to-one mentoring, she counts it a privilege to walk alongside others on their journeys.

Kerry has her B.R.E. degree from Peace River Bible Institute, has worked in the non-profit world for more than 26 years, and shared her first author experience in *Carried: 10 Stories of Finding Supernatural Peace in the Midst of Pain and Confusion.*

Kerry resides in central Alberta along with her husband of 32 years. They love spending time with their three adult sons and newly acquired daughter-in-law by camping and playing board games. When she is not working or involved in encouraging others, Kerry loves keeping her husband busy with hiking, biking, golfing, or walking their energetic dog Vinnie.

To contact Kerry to speak at your event you can go to wwmm.ca or klrobi50@gmail.com.

REST AND REFLECTION DAYS

E very seven days, we have inserted a Rest and Reflection day. This is a day that you can journal, interact with us, or simply rest.

We will have prompts for you to follow and suggestions on ways to relax or pray… or both. Grab a notebook to write down your thoughts, or scribble away in the book.

We hope that these are profitable days in your journey. Days of healing and hope.

Please feel free to share your R and R days with us and send us your thoughts on these days at wwmmconnect@gmail.com.

We would love to hear from you!

WWMM Team

SPIRITUAL SEASONS

Lynda Blazina

"Praise be to the name of God for ever and ever; wisdom and power are his. He changes times and seasons; he deposes kings and raises up others. He gives wisdom to the wise and knowledge to the discerning. He reveals deep and hidden things; he knows what lies in darkness, and light dwells with him. I thank and praise you, God of my ancestors: You have given me wisdom and power, you have made known to me what we asked of you, you have made known to us the dream of the king" (Dan 2:20–21).

Seasons change. In the natural world we know this, expect this; we anticipate and sometimes even dread the change of seasons. But we know that the change of seasons will occur, especially for those blessed to live in an area of drastic seasonal changes like I do.

Summer is my favourite season. I anticipate the warmth and activity of the summer months. I enjoy sitting by the pool, basking in the sun, enjoying time off from the regular routine of kids being in school. I enjoy the summer activities of camping, hiking, gardening, and being on the back deck, barbecuing with friends and family.

Winter is hard for me. On top of the cold and snow, which I struggle to find a reason why God would create, the lack of sunlight during the winter months affects my mood and demeanour. For the vast majority of my life, I have dreaded winter. I dread it so much, in fact, that I have a hard time enjoying fall because I know that my favourite season is done and winter is on its way!

It's much the same in my spiritual life. Until recent years, I had been blessed with mostly spiritual summer. There were thunderstorms that would blow through to be sure, but in general, it was sunny skies in the forecast. Then a few years ago winter fell, and fell hard. Since then, it seems that I have been stuck fluctuating between winter and fall for many seasons.

This has made me as uncomfortable in my spiritual walk as I would be in my physical life had I been transported against my will to live out my days in the Antarctic! And, I'll be honest, I've struggled with finding God's reasoning for placing so much winter in my spiritual life.

I have had to work through reconciling the God of summer with the God of winter. How can the God who loves me so much that He was willing to give everything—including His very life—for my salvation, also be the God who not only allows, but sometimes makes things happen in my life that are painful and the cause of great suffering?

It was scary to believe that God was actually in control of the things that were tearing my life apart. It was terrifying to think that He wasn't!

To believe that God is in control of pain, suffering, and loss also means that, just as with seasons, there is purpose and design to them. Even though winter has settled in, I worship the God who changes seasons, who knows what lies in darkness, and who deposes kings and sets new ones in place.

Think about that! That is a source of such deep hope. God has a purpose and a plan for everything He has designed, which means He has purpose and use for every moment of pain you have walked through. Through the work of the Holy Spirit, He has the power to use everything you have experienced for His glory.

Recently, my family has taken up skiing. It's something to do in the winter that helps me be a little less miserable about the cold and snow. One day, I was out with my son who absolutely loves snowboarding and spends many hours on the mountain. There was a moment, as we were sitting in the quiet on the chairlift together, that I looked at him and had a profound realization. I had found a precious treasure of time with my son...because of winter!

What season are you in? Maybe you are walking through a season of fall and dreading that another long winter might be ahead of you. You might be wading through hip-deep snow, or possibly even be in a season of spring or summer with a winter behind you.

Walk with us as we share some of the lessons and truths we have learned through great trials and struggles and discover the depth of hope that runs through every season God has designed. We hope that you will find treasures of love, hope, joy, peace, perseverance, God's goodness, and deep faith. We also pray that, through our stories, God will reveal deep and hidden things of Himself to you.

HOPE DEFERRED

Charleen Raschke

Deferred: "postponed or delayed"
(Dictionary.com, 2018)

"Hope deferred makes the heart sick…" (Prov 13:12).

It was January 2005: the middle of winter in every way. Darkness was nearly swallowing our family. We were surviving, sure, but barely. Our wounded souls were crying out for rescue, for deliverance. *Where are You, God?* My head told me He was there, but my heart could not feel His warmth or His presence.

How does one hang on in the recoil of such evil, such despair? We were wrestling with our God of love and compassion as the knowledge that He is loving stood in stark contrast to what we were experiencing. If He is all-powerful, how could He allow this to happen? How was my mind to comprehend that He could have intervened, but chose not to?

The darkened days of winter mirrored the darkened days of our souls. Hope only came for brief moments, if at all. If hope deferred does indeed make hearts sick, we were in deep trouble. *Oh, God, where are You?*

2 Samuel 13 tells the story of Tamar, King David's beautiful daughter, who was tricked and then raped by her half-brother Amnon. When David found out what his son had done to his daughter, the Bible tells us that he was furious. After two years Tamar's brother Absalom, who

had obviously not forgotten the shame and pain inflicted upon his sister, devised a plan to finally have Amnon killed.

If you remove the brother-raping-his-own-sister part of this story, it is way too close to home for our family. Our beautiful, barely 15-year-old daughter was tricked, drugged, and then brutally raped. The furious father was my husband. The brother with murderous thoughts was my son.

Pain and heartache were our close companions. Our faith was tested in so many ways. How could we ever hope again?

I'd love to say we all had a miraculous moment and everything evil was erased, but that isn't how things unfolded for us. It was one excruciating tiny step after another. Sometimes we stepped backwards instead of forwards. Because of the time our healing took, there were many moments when hope felt unkindly postponed. Eventually we found breathing easier.

We were surrounded by praying people. This was of incredible value to our family—knowing we did not have to go through this alone. We were also immersed in weekly counselling for a long season. Our godly counsellor held us up many times with her wisdom as she led us into forgiveness and taught us to let go of our pain.

If you've been in a pain-filled season and you feel at a loss for where to turn, I encourage you to not give up! Keep hanging on, even if it's by a thread. If at all possible, contact friends and family who will pray for you and get connected to a counsellor you can trust.

God has never left you. He promised He would never leave you or forsake you (Deut 31:6). He hears your cries; He catches your tears. You can cry out to Him.

CELEBRATING A STAR

Kerry Robideau

"The sun has one kind of splendor, the moon another and the stars another; and star differs from star in splendor" (1 Cor 15:41).

A good friend once said to me, in the early stages of our relationship, "I can't relate to you; you're too perfect." I wanted to look perfect. I wanted people to think that I, as a young pastor's wife, had it all together. I thought others would like me more and be more attracted to me if I upheld the image of having it all together and having all the answers. I was a person who always wanted to be seen as having done right and able to help others, but here I was being confronted with my own strategy of survival.

My friend was right. No one would come to me because no one could relate to me. I wasn't real. God opened my eyes that day and started me on a lifelong path of becoming more authentic in my life and faith.

Obedience in this area, however, later led to awkwardness and misunderstanding. It came at a time in our lives when God was asking my husband and me to share our true realities, our struggles and our weaknesses. It was a call to us and to our church to be vulnerable and loving to each other. Instead, we were minimized; told that we were weak, flawed, and not fit for ministry. We were crushed. My husband was my example of authenticity. He knew how to just be himself and people, young and old alike, loved him. Now I watched him disappear as the hurt and rejection deepened. The few who saw him as weak worked relentlessly to have him removed. It broke us, and we left feeling unloved. We had done lots of counselling for broken marriages in the past and this felt like a nasty divorce, where one side wanted to work things out and the other had no interest in any kind of reconciliation.

In the midst of this, God opened the door for us to attend a retreat for broken leaders involved in ministry. One of the men who was there to help us with healing asked us if we would be his example of working through the issues of pain and rejection. We agreed. He had us sit on the floor with big foam blocks in different sizes, shapes and colours, and asked us to share our story. The blocks became our playing pieces. The only block that still stands out to me was one shaped like a V. It was a large thick block and we said it stood for vulnerability. That's what got us into trouble.

Then a listener pointed out to us that the size of the block was significant. Vulnerability wasn't a flaw or a weakness, but a huge strength! That insight changed our outlook on what had taken place. We were right in sharing. We were right in being who God called us to be that day.

"While 'one star differs from another star in glory' (1 Cor 15:41), God calls all the stars by name and He keeps count of them (Ps 147:4; Isa 40:26). Some stars show obvious differences in color and brightness. Others require spectroscopic study to detect their particular identity or fingerprint. All the heavenly bodies pursue their assigned paths; each has its name and place, and each has its role in the great procession of space. The Creator has displayed infinite wisdom and power in marshaling the countless hosts of stars and in guiding and keeping them in their particular spheres" (BibleAsk.org).

I took what my friend told me years ago to heart. God has shown me over and over again that people are drawn in when I am who God created me to be. God made us just like the stars, to shine our splendour in all its glory. He's made each of us unique in our personalities, our likes and dislikes, our interests, our favourites, the things we are attracted to, the ways we like to have fun, our intellects, our physical beings, and the ways in which we love others. All of these aspects are meant to reflect His beautiful image to a lost and hopeless world.

Celebrate you—shine like a star!

KNOWING GOD BY ACCIDENT

Deborah Carpenter

The snow falling. The flashing lights of the fire trucks, police cars, and ambulances reflecting into the wet, foggy haze. Watching traffic redirected past an accident, trying to see what had happened. Emergency responders waiting for their turn to help. Organized chaos. And somewhere in the middle of it all, my husband. Trapped inside a mangled truck. Unconscious and waiting to be rescued.

And me. Standing outside in the cold, wet spring snow. My shoes soaked and my mind numb. A coldness deep in my chest. He is alive, the policeman said. Alive? Meaning what, exactly? Not dead? I could not comprehend. You should call someone. Like who? And tell them what?

Somewhere deep within my mind, a thought formed. One single thought. Like a question, but not. Perhaps it was a 'knowing.' A glimmer of hope. A truth to stand on, phrased like a questioning child seeking affirmation of what they've been told is true. Please, please be true. If the God I serve is not sovereign, if He is not in complete control of this chaos, if His hand is not at work somehow, somewhere in all this, then there is no future; I am lost.

There are defining moments in our lives. Abrupt and jarring moments that we did not see coming. Moments whose impact is felt long after the shock waves have dissipated. Moments that reveal to us who God truly is and reveal to us who we truly are. We can trip over these moments and come to the wrong conclusions. Both Job and Jonah had one of these moments.

In Jonah's case he had heard from God, but he chose to deliberately disobey Him—and was swallowed by a whale. His moment came in the belly of a whale.

Jonah prays: "When my life was fainting away, I remembered the LORD, and my prayer came to you, into your holy temple…Salvation belongs to the LORD!"

God's answer: "And the LORD spoke to the fish, and it vomited Jonah out upon the dry land." Jonah proceeds in obedience to God's command to go to Nineveh.

In Job's case, he accused God of being unjust as he felt he was suffering terrible things even though he was a righteous man. His moment came in the ash heap.

Job prays: "I cry out to you, God, but you do not answer; I stand up, but you merely look at me. You turn on me ruthlessly" (Job 30:20–21a).

God's answer: "Shall a faultfinder contend with the Almighty? He who argues with God, let him answer it" (Job 40:2).

These two men had their own characters revealed in the presence of this one true God. Both realized their own limited understanding of God. Jonah thought he could hide. Job thought God was ignoring his plight. Unfortunately Jonah forgot, or never realized, that the very God who showed him mercy and delivered him from certain death would want to do the same for the Ninevites. We leave him sitting under a wilted tree lamenting the mercy God showed to the city of Nineveh. He is unhappy about who God revealed Himself to be.

Job, for his part, wisely throws himself on the mercy of God; in his wisdom, he answers Him, "Behold, I am of small account." He repents "in dust and ashes" as he comes face to face with his limited understanding of God. We leave Job with all he had lost doubly restored. Job must have spent the rest of his life worshipping God as God had revealed Himself to be.

How these men responded to God is less of the story. The real story is who God revealed Himself to be. Kind and compassionate. Slow to anger. Merciful in all His ways. A God who will not act unjustly towards the righteous, regardless of how it seems to them. In their distress, both men called out to God. While their circumstances and prayers were different, they were both calling on the same God. And they both heard from God.

Perhaps you have had a moment like this. A moment that caught you by surprise. Perhaps you aren't as surprised by the circumstance you find yourself in as you are surprised by a God who allowed it to happen. Who is this God who has men swallowed by whales and stripped of everything except their own life?! Who is this God who allows trucks to career out of control on a highway and cancer to form in the bodies of those we love? Disillusionment strikes hard and fast. How are we to respond to a God like this in the middle of our worst days?

As I stood on the side of the highway, I too called out to God. Everything I knew about Him would be tested against my own flawed character. I would need to cling ever tightly to who God truly was and not who I wanted Him to be.

I knew I was of very small account.

And yet it felt as though, with that admission, the God of the universe was stooping down to take my hand.

WHO AM I?

Connie Lucille Peachey

L iving in a small town is like living in a fishbowl. Everyone knows everything about everyone. Being in the ministry, in a small church, in a small town, is like being naked inside that fishbowl. Living with nothing hidden. People see how real I am, how human. There's no way to be consistently fake. But my 'authentic' is so disappointing for some. They want someone who does things the way they should be done. By that, they often mean someone who is always available, who sees their every difficulty as an emergency, and who is ready to come at the drop of a hat.

Growing up with an aversion to disappointing people, I set myself up for failure and burnout. It's almost impossible to be authentic when you are afraid of disappointing people. Someone will always be disappointed.

For many years it wasn't safe for me to be Connie. She was too loud, too bossy, too opinionated, too much! And also, not enough. Connie was not quiet enough, gentle enough, or submissive enough. Eventually I lost Connie. I no longer knew who she was or what was important to her. I was ruled by the desire to 'not disappoint people.'

Many times I am introduced as 'our pastor's wife' without anyone giving my name. I am invited to places because I am a pastor's wife. Doors open and close to me on the basis of whom I am married to. I am not really seen as a woman or even a person but rather as 'other'; like the box you check when nothing else fits; like an ornament on their pastor's arm. 'Pastor's wife' is the title/identity that has trumped all the others for most of my adult life.

A few years ago we entered a season of ambivalence and anonymity. We took a leave of absence from pastoral ministry. Who was Connie when she was not married to the pastor? What value did she have? What purpose was she created for?

Then when we did enter the ministry again it was in a place where the pastor's wife was not seen as a vital part of the ministry team. Now I was really lost.

The dictionary definition of **identity** (compilation from Oxford, Merriam–Webster, Cambridge) is "the fact of being who or what a person or thing is; individuality, character, distinctiveness; qualities, beliefs; the way a person thinks and operates; the qualities that make a person uniquely them."

This is Dr. Rob Reimer's definition in his book *Soul Care*: "What you believe about yourself is the foundation of your life; it is your identity."

My identity: wife, mother, nana, pastor's wife, music teacher, author, writer, friend, sister, daughter, opinionated, leader, ambivert, woman, warrior, passionate Jesus-follower, loved by God.

Recently, a series of unfortunate events forced me to embark on a journey through a deep, dark valley where God had my undivided attention. During this time He became more real to me than ever before. I began to see Connie as He sees Connie. I began to let myself off the hook of expectations because I could not deliver, and He seemed to be okay with that.

As, one by one, things were stripped away I began to realize that my significance was not in what I did or did not do, who I knew, what my husband did for a living, or what role I played. God was after my heart.

The book of Ephesians is one of the best passages of Scripture to read if you are struggling with your own sense of worth or identity. Here are some truths gleaned from chapter 1:

He [God] blessed us (v. 3)
He loved us (v. 4)
He chose us (vv. 4, 11)
He adopted us (v. 5)
We belong to His Son (v. 6)
He showers us with kindness (v. 8)
He gives us an inheritance (v. 11)
He identifies us as His own (v. 13)
He gave us His own Holy Spirit (v. 13)
He purchased us to be His own (v. 14)

The only qualifiers on these blessings are that we must believe Jesus Christ is God's Son, that He came in the flesh, and that He paid the price for our sins (v. 13). Personality, position, race and gender do not factor into this in any way.

When I can operate from these truths, I can fully live out my identity, my personality, my role and my calling. My true identity is not in any of these but rather in whom I belong to and who has proclaimed my inestimable value. I am a child of the one true King. Nothing can alter that! Nothing and no one can steal that.

"He [God] has identified us as his own by placing the Holy Spirit in our hearts as the first installment that guarantees everything he has promised us" (2 Cor 1:22, NLT).

"You are a chosen people…God's very own possession" (1 Pet 2:9, NLT).

What freedom to be released from having to perform in a certain way to be accepted and feel valued. We have nothing to prove because God has already proved that His love for us is unshakeable. Why would we trade that for the fickle praise of man?

Don't get me wrong: I like to be liked. I still struggle with disappointing people. However, I have learned that our value and identity are not dependent on what others think or say about us. The solid foundation of our true identity is found in what God says about us, and He has written it down for us in case we forget!

Do you want to walk in freedom from striving for approval? Do you long to *belong*? Then I invite you to believe what God says about you in His Word. Read the above list again, this time with your name in it.

You are dearly loved. You belong.

GUILT TO VICTORY

Lisa Clarke

Carrying guilt for events that happen in our lives, even things that were out of our control, can create years of anxiety and exhaustion. I can attest to this, especially in the last five years. I carried guilt over things left unsaid with my daughter before she passed away, guilt in my marriage, guilt over never being able to complete everything on my plate with my family, guilt over not staying in touch with people over the years, and the list goes on.

I imagine we all carry guilt of some kind, for various circumstances, that eats us up inside. Satan loves nothing more than to parade our guilt before us and remind us of how much we have failed others. He continually tries to whisper guilt and shame in our ears.

However, in Ephesians 2:5 God says that He has "made us alive with Christ even when we were dead in transgressions—it is by grace you have been saved." In this verse, God shows us the remarkable truth that He is for us and we are His workmanship.

Because of His love and mercy through Jesus Christ, God has made a way for us to rest in His grace. The enemy wants us to believe we are dead in transgressions, but God reminds us in this verse that we are alive with Christ.

Romans 8:1 says that "there is now no condemnation for those in Christ Jesus."

Guilt and regret can keep us in a prison of pain and solitude. The enemy wants us to feel alone, and often works to alienate us so we become discouraged or feel unloved. It is also easy to surround ourselves with others who struggle and who can bring us into a pit of guilt with them; however, we can find freedom from our guilt through the amazing forgiveness of Jesus.

He waits to release us from our guilt as we realize that His forgiveness is complete and we are complete in Him. When we are in Him, we wear His righteousness and there is no longer condemnation for the failures that we carry with us.

Because of God's grace we are free.

Rest in that truth as you read through Romans 8:31–39:

"What then shall we say to these things? If God is for us, who can be against us? He who did not spare his own Son but gave him up for us all, how will he not also with him graciously give us all things? Who shall bring any charge against God's elect? It is God who justifies. Who is to condemn? Christ Jesus is the one who died—more than that, who was raised—who is at the right hand of God, who indeed is interceding for us.

"Who shall separate us from the love of Christ? Shall tribulation, or distress, or persecution, or famine, or nakedness, or danger, or sword? As it is written, 'For your sake we are being killed all the day long; we are regarded as sheep to be slaughtered.' No, in all these things we are more than conquerors through him who loved us. For I am sure that neither death nor life, nor angels nor rulers, nor things present nor things to come, nor powers, nor height nor depth, nor anything else in all creation, will be able to separate us from the love of God in Christ Jesus our Lord."

If you are searching Scripture and crying out to God as you feel a burden of guilt or shame—I don't say this lightly—trust God! My hope for you is that you rely more on Jesus than on yourself; that you can bring your guilt and shame to the cross and lay it down at Jesus' feet. You are loved by God more than you can possibly know.

REST AND REFLECTION

Your Name

What is the devotional from the last few days that you identify with most?

Why?

If you were to write a devotional based on an emotion what would it be?

Journal about your experiences with this emotion.

FOR SUCH A TIME

Brenda Goudy

"**B**eing confident of this, that he who began a good work in you will carry it on to completion until the day of Christ Jesus" (Phil 1:6).

Food and friends. Give me a free day and that is how I will fill my time. There's nothing I enjoy more than catching up with friends over a good cup of coffee or a delicious meal. It's even better if we can go out and be served, so that no one is responsible for cleaning up! I have learned to keep friend time precious and a priority, as other responsibilities will weigh down my time if I let them.

I have a friend who has walked alongside me for many years. She was my 'sister' throughout my difficult marriage, and has supported me (together with her husband and sons) in practical ways that have assuaged my worries and built my self-esteem. We meet weekly for half-price appetizers at a neighbourhood restaurant to make sure our connection stays strong. Sometimes we invite others; sometimes we keep it 'just us.'

She knows my insecurities and my strengths. And I know hers. We encourage, support, and help each other get through life's difficulties. We have weathered health concerns, my troubled marriage, struggles with our children, family issues, and job challenges over the years. And we have laughed—a lot. When the opportunity for me to become involved in this writing project came up, all my insecurities also came to visit. As I shared this with her, her face lit up with joy and encouragement and I knew I was not going to have any excuse to avoid taking up this new challenge.

And then she said something that turned my hesitation into motivation.

"Brenda," she said, "This is what God had planned for you all along. There are things that have kept you from becoming who God intended you to be for a long time, but they never changed God's plan for you."

God's plan for me may have been delayed by many years, by hardship and distraction, but it never changed. He knew all along that I would come to this place and finally be ready and available to surrender to His leading.

I often think of Queen Esther in the Bible, and of her years of delay. She was chosen to be a new queen, based on little more than her beauty (Esther 2). Even though she was chosen as a beautiful woman, she had to undergo a year of beauty treatments before being presented to the king. Thrown into a life where she was now part of a harem, I'm sure she wondered how she had ended up in that place. But God had a bigger purpose in mind. The king chose her to be his queen.

Even then, her full purpose was delayed until the time was right. When the time came (Esther 4) and her uncle came up with a plan in which she would beg her husband, the king, to save the Jewish people, Esther was afraid. She knew the laws of the land, and she knew she would be taking a huge risk. I'm sure she was terrified, as the punishment for initiating a conversation with the king could be death.

There was no guarantee that she would be successful or that she would be granted mercy. It had been a month since she had last seen him; any woman in her situation would worry that she had been forgotten! Then her uncle made a wise observation.

"Do not think that because you are in the king's house you alone of all the Jews will escape. For if you remain silent at this time, relief and deliverance for the Jews will arise from another place, but you and your father's family will perish. And who knows but that you have come to your royal position for such a time as this?" (Esther 4:12–14).

For such a time as this. God's plan for Esther never changed. It was there all along. It was delayed by beauty treatments, delayed by a marriage to an unbeliever, even delayed when she initially approached the king, but it never changed. Esther took the risk and saved her people.

It's a risk for me to fully engage in my writing project. I could fail. My insecurities could take over and delay my involvement, but God has a plan that hasn't changed. It will never change. Prayer and encouragement from friends and loved ones have pushed me to take the risk. As opportunities arise, all of us will have decisions to make. As God leads, we will have to choose to take the risk and follow Him, or delay our submission to His leading. Yet through it all, His purposes will be fulfilled, and His plan will not change.

ROLLER COASTERS

Ryshon Blazina

As long as I can remember, I always hated roller coasters. I don't like to be scared, so why would I do that to myself intentionally?

This week, I found I was ready for the week to be over before it had even begun. That mindset put me on a roller coaster—continually up and down emotionally and, in the end, right back on the ground where I had started.

Romans 5:3–5 (ESV) says:

"Not only that, but we rejoice in our sufferings, knowing that suffering produces character, and character produces hope, and hope does not put us to shame, because God's love has been poured into our hearts through the Holy Spirit who has been given to us."

I get it that sometimes the circumstances that come up in life really, really suck. It's okay to allow yourself to feel the emotions of those things and walk through them; however, it's also a scary temptation to allow yourself to get stuck in a place of hurt, self-pity, and distress.

Even when it doesn't feel like it, God's grace and peace are strong enough to get you off the roller coaster. Personally, I want to start focusing on and thinking about things that are going to push me forward, to new places, closer to my destiny in Christ. I want to avoid the roller coasters. As Romans says, I want my suffering to produce and develop my character, and I want my hope to be secure in God's love and in His Holy Spirit in my life.

CHANGES

Stefanie Carlson

"My thoughts are nothing like your thoughts," says the LORD. "And my ways are far beyond anything you could imagine. For just as the heavens are higher than the earth, so my ways are higher than your ways and my thoughts higher than your thoughts" (Isa 55:8–9, NLT).

My husband Drew and I hired a nanny after our youngest daughter was born, three and a half years ago. She was an amazing Filipino woman who came into our lives and just made them better. She was like a third parent and a grandma all at once. She took care of all of us. Having her as a part of our lives gave me the ability to really focus on my business, and having her support in our home permitted amazing success.

So it came as an unbelievable shock this past fall when Mary announced her resignation with only two weeks' notice. My husband and I were both pained with an overwhelming feeling of loss. I tried to be positive even when sharing the news with family and friends.

I always try to understand situations from other perspectives, and I knew that as my babies turned into children, the tasks required of Mary had changed. I always assumed she would grow and change with us. However, sometimes it takes painful disappointment to teach us something, and I believe that God's timing is perfect.

"For I know the plans I have for you," says the LORD.

"They are plans for good and not for disaster, to give you a future and a hope" (Jer 29:11, NLT).

Understanding Mary's perspective didn't change my emotional response, however. My anxiety was coupled with feelings of abandonment. I was also at a loss. I had full-time clients, a husband in school, and two weeks to figure out a new normal.

Through a lot of prayer (and many panic attacks) we found a fitting replacement, and both Drew and I had peace about our decision.

"Don't worry about anything; instead, pray about everything. Tell God what you need, and thank him for all he has done. Then you will experience God's peace, which exceeds anything we can understand. His peace will guard your hearts and minds as you live in Christ Jesus" (Phil 4:6–7, NLT).

We cannot get through life without experiencing change. Sometimes it knocks the wind right out of us. Change is even more difficult when it's imposed on us suddenly or without our approval.

As time passed with Mary gone, I noticed characteristics in my oldest daughter that I hadn't noticed before. She began to open up to me in a new and honest way. She said she felt safe. These words from my then six-year-old woke my spirit to pay attention. I looked at her, and I saw that she had been wounded. She showed signs of being very self-conscious and lacking in confidence. My heart broke, looking at her and seeing her in this way and not knowing why.

All I could do was softly and gently speak life over her. I told her over and over, "I am so happy that you feel safe and loved." I believed that if I spoke intentionally to my little girl, her crushed spirit would be strengthened and come to life.

"The soothing tongue is a tree of life, but a perverse tongue crushes the spirit" (Prov 15:4, NLT).

As time passed, I watched as Lyric began to break free from her dark cloud of shame. She started telling me the secrets that she had kept from us when our previous nanny was with us. The secret that she had been exposed to adult television. That she had been hit and pinched by Mary, and that she was constantly put down verbally.

"The LORD is near to the brokenhearted and saves the crushed in spirit" (Ps 34:18, ESV).

Grief and anger stuck to me like black, sticky tar. I was in complete disbelief that this person I thought I knew, and whom I fully trusted with the safekeeping and wellbeing of my children, was not who I thought she was. It happened before my eyes, yet behind closed doors, all the while slowly wounding my little girl's soul. I felt outraged by the realization that Mary was not who she was expected or believed to be.

"Weeping may last through the night, but joy comes with the morning (Ps 30:5, NLT).

If Mary had never given us her resignation, the abuse both physically and mentally would have continued. I would like to say that eventually I would have noticed, but shame is a terrible thing, and even the small signs I did recognize I swept away as challenges with grade school, changing schedules, or simply growing up.

The things that we think are happening *to* us may actually be happening *for* us—like Mary handing in her resignation.

As we began our family's journey into inner healing and began to see our bruises heal, we learned very valuable lessons.

"Don't worry about anything; instead, pray about everything. Tell God what you need, and thank him for all he has done. Then you will experience God's peace, which exceeds anything we can understand. His peace will guard your hearts and minds as you live in Christ Jesus" (Phil 4:6–7, NLT).

JUST HOLD ME

Charleen Raschke

The phone rang. As I placed the receiver down, I needed to find a spot to crumble. Our basement was ideal. I found my spot and allowed grief to envelop me. I didn't fight it. Wave upon wave of emotion came crashing down on me. My uncle was in a fight for his life and I could feel it.

His heart was in very bad condition. We were not sure if he would make it through the surgery or even through the night. The seriousness of it weighed on me. I wasn't even that close to him, so the depth of grief that hit me was surprising. It may have had to do with experiencing very little loss until this point in my life.

The tears and grief felt necessary and appropriate. So I went there. Deep sobs followed by more deep sobs.

My husband came down for a few moments, but the discomfort he felt in situations like this was no different this time. I think he felt inadequate. If he couldn't fix what was wrong, he was at a loss. So, after a very brief hug, he escaped the uncomfortable place that my grief had created. I wished he would have stayed, but he wasn't really sure how to help. He didn't realize that 'help' was not what I wanted or needed at that moment.

It was then that my young teenage son came downstairs. He was bold and he was brave. He didn't say much more than that he was sorry and that he loved me. That was all. No more words.

He sat beside me on the floor for what seemed to be a very long time. He held me as my tears fell. It was healing. It was needed. It was kind.

Often, because of our upbringing or simply our culture, we see someone in pain or grief and do not know what to do or what to say. The problem is usually that we want to 'fix' the situation. More often than not, fixing isn't applicable or even possible in these scenarios.

That day, I needed to be supported in the way of a simple hug. I needed to be supported in the act of being there. Grief needs to be felt. It's an act that needs to flow freely from us.

If it were a physical wound, we would not say to the person, "Stop feeling that—it's making me uncomfortable!" But our actions often communicate that message to people in emotional pain.

"Rejoice with those who rejoice, and weep with those who weep" (Rom 12:15, NASB).

That's fairly clear. It seems easy and acceptable to do the rejoicing part; however, in our society, the weeping portion has a tone of being uncomfortable and awkward.

Recently I was discussing this topic with my son's fiancée. She had some insight that I felt was profound. She said, "I always imagined that when someone would hug like that as a response it was like they were trying to take some of that pain away."

It's time for change. It's time for us to usher in a healthy view of grief. Let's embrace learning how to do this well.

BE STILL

Lynda Blazina

More drama. More pain. More confusion as I watch my child struggling to fight through a new web of their own design. I wonder what I need to do to help them break through the strands that are gripping and holding them down.

With my children's struggles come emotional struggles of my own. Feelings of guilt, frustration, helplessness, worry, impatience—to name but a few.

I know that God is at work. I see it; I feel it. I've been praying for Him to intervene and I know that I pray to a God who hears me. But oh, how I wish that He would hurry up! I see opportunities in everything, and with each new circumstance feel that 'it' would be a perfect chance for God to intervene. Please God do a miracle through this… okay, maybe *this*?

But no Damascus Road experiences. No switching on of a lightbulb. No waking up and having my once-wandering child now an evangelist with a desire to change the world.

I find myself wanting to manipulate situations so that God's voice will be heard by my seemingly deaf child. I fight the urge to turn up the Christian songs that come on the radio to decibels that would shake their body, if not their soul. I want to arrange meetings with people who have had life-changing experiences that I just *know* God would want my child to emulate. I want to ask people that have life-altering experiences with God to take my kid under their wing and show them how they too could be changed.

I feel the pressure to handle every situation with kid gloves, hearing the criticism from others before it's ever spoken. Sometimes I recognize the voice of criticism as my own perfectionism and feelings that my child's actions are a byproduct of my own shortcomings in parenting and human-ing. Have you heard them? "If only I had ... Why didn't I ... I shouldn't have ... Maybe then ..."

But the whispers to my soul are "Be still and know that I am God" (Ps 46:10, NIV) and "Wait for the LORD; be strong and take heart and wait for the LORD" (Ps 27:14).

Be still.

I used to read this verse with a very pastoral and serene inner voice. Rest in Me and know I am God. I am the big pillow you can lay your head on and know that all will be okay. Rest, relax, enjoy the scenery, smell the roses, knowing you can cast all your cares on Me or out the window... You get the idea.

Lately though, that sweet inner voice has got an edge to it! It's turned from a restful and peaceful idea that this weary soul gravitates toward into more of a command. *Be still!* Quit moving. Stop doing. Stop trying to figure it all out, stop trying to force the situation into one that you can handle and take care of and control the outcome of.

... And know that I am God.

Have you ever put the em-PHAS-is on the wrong syl-LA-ble? That's what I was doing with this portion of the verse. I was reading it as KNOW that I am GOD. Rest assured you have your confidence in the right place. I'm your Superhero who will sweep in and save the day. Know that I can do anything.

Although that is all true, the emphasis the small quiet voice—now a persistent boom in my head—was trying to convey was this: Not you. ME. I am God. I am the one who changes lives. I am the one who can soften hearts. I am the truth that can realign the trajectory of a human soul. Did you get that? Not *you* ... Me. I AM.

Wait for the Lord.

Wait on the Lord's perfect timing. He is the one in control of time and space. He is the one who not only sees the future but designs it. Why do we try so desperately to guess what the whole picture is when we've only been given one little piece of the puzzle? Be patient. Wait.

Be strong and take heart.

Again with the commands! This turned from a nicety—a mere suggestion—to a military command. These are MY instructions in the battle. Be strong. Don't sit there waiting for the possibility of maybe something sort of good happening. Be strong. Do battle. Pray. Wait. Battle. Fight. Learn. Grow, and take heart.

Because I know that I am not strong alone, and yet I am commanded to be strong, I have to assume I am not alone in the battle. I can take heart because God walks with me in it all.

Wait for the Lord.

The fact that this is repeated twice is not insignificant to me. I don't think any of us are particularly wired to enjoy hardship. It's not in the blueprint of how we were created. When trials and pain do come our way, it's a natural response to try to get through it as quickly as possible. But again, the Lord who is in control of the universe says…wait.

These are not lessons easily learned or mastered. I am constantly in a battle between my own desires and wishes and trying to follow through with the lessons I see and learn as God speaks to me through His Word. But His Word is living and true and when I live out the life-giving lessons of Scripture, I am able to truly be still and know that He is God.

A MIRACLE IN MONS

Bethany Buchnor

For the last seven years I have been the nomadic wife of a professional basketball player. From Argentina to Germany to Belgium and now back in Germany, we have packed and unpacked many a home. We have made wonderful memories but planted no roots. And we never know what's around the corner.

After three years in Germany, my husband's career landed us in Mons, Belgium.

I arrived with feelings of excitement and adventure, but was very quickly disillusioned. My husband's schedule was very busy and required a lot of travelling throughout Europe. I had no friends, no community, and nothing to do. I was at home, often alone, with a then two-year-old son and six-month-old daughter.

My days consisted of a morning walk around the city, lunch and nap time back home, and an afternoon walk around the city, retracing the exact same lonely steps of the morning. My loneliness began to envelop me. Motherhood alone can be isolating anyway—add being in a foreign country, unable to communicate with anyone and having no clue where to begin, and I quickly reached a stalemate within. I couldn't last an entire year like this.

One rainy January afternoon I told my husband that I was not okay. I decided to go for a walk and out for coffee to collect my thoughts. My husband saw the deep discontentment in my eyes and began to pray.

I wandered around the lonely cobblestone streets of Belgium, seeing everything through a filter of self-pity. I was stuck in my thoughts, seeing no light or beauty in my surroundings. I wandered to a coffeehouse I knew of, hoping to sit and relax. When I arrived it was closed. I thought of another so I headed there, only to find it closed as well. I thought of one more option, an American coffeehouse my sister had discovered while visiting us at Christmas. I remembered that they had free Wi-Fi and peanut butter mochas, so I decided to make my way there. I ordered a drink, a sweet treat, and sat down in the back to be to be by myself.

The woman who owned the coffeehouse arrived with my order. I remember her walking over with a big smile and true southern charm. As she placed my coffee down, she said, "Here you go. It's great to see you. How are you?"

In that moment I resisted the urge to answer with a generic, "Thank you, I'm good." I found comfort in the kindness of this stranger, and felt that I had nothing to lose.

I answered, "Actually, I'm *not* good."

The woman sat down across from me and I unloaded. I explained what had brought me to this random French Belgian city, listed my struggles, expressed my pessimism, and confessed my loneliness.

She listened with intent and welcomed my honesty with grace. After about ten minutes of handing her a platter of messy and muddled emotion, I asked, "So what brought *you* here?"

She smiled. After a moment of hesitation, she replied, "My husband and I are actually missionaries. We've come to Mons to help women come out of trafficking."

In that moment my entire body was awakened. I had goosebumps on my arms, and a cloud was instantly lifted. I looked at her, completely gobsmacked, and said "I am a Christian. I have volunteered with trafficking organizations for years—my heart is *so* there!"

Her eyes widened and we both exhaled with gratitude. She explained more of her vision for the coffeehouse and specifics of their ministry. I asked if she had a church. She said yes, and explained that the NATO base not far from where we were had a chapel they attended.

Not only that, but the pastor's wife was volunteering at the coffeehouse at that moment. Nicole, this woman who now had a name, called her over to join us.

I had walked into that coffeehouse feeling immense isolation, and now, here I was, sitting with sisters. We laughed and began to share more of our lives and our stories. Minutes turned into hours. They told me they would get me a pass for the NATO base so I could attend chapel. They told me there was a women's ministry beginning the next week with free childcare. They told me of English playgroups and children's activities I was welcome to attend.

My heart was bursting. I decided to go home and get my family and come right back. When I walked into our apartment and saw my husband, I began talking a mile a minute. He looked at me in amazement. He told me he had been praying. He couldn't believe the difference between the person I was when I left versus the person I was now. We packed up the kids and spent the next couple of hours with our new friends at the Texas coffeehouse in Mons, Belgium.

From that day on, everything changed. We began attending the chapel. I joined the women's ministry and was invited to lead worship. I had opportunities to work with victims of human trafficking. God knew my truest self, and He provided a community that saw me at my core. I was welcomed with open arms to an incredible community of Christian military wives. These women were all used to a nomadic lifestyle, all fellow 'fish out of water' in this little Belgian city. We were in this together. We were sisters.

Our life in Belgium faced endless challenges. Every appliance in our apartment broke, my husband suffered multiple sports injuries, and I had my own gamut of health issues including two emergency root canals. Then, with a two-year-old son and a ten-month-old daughter, I found myself pregnant yet again.

While all of this was very challenging, it was a truly incredible time in our lives. My soul was fed and I was given life. It made me better. It refocused me. Our experience in Mons became a powerful reminder of grace and surrender. Grace awaits us in every darkness, in every downpour. To-day, I look back and smile, considering how I once dismissed this place as dull and gloomy. This place was a gift, a treasure, whose streets are vibrant and sacred to me now. My anthem during this time was a beautiful song, written by Tracy Rahn, called "Dancing in the Downpour."

The chorus is as follows:

So when it rains I won't run undercover
And when it floods I won't head for the hills
When the lightning sets dark skies on fire
I will raise up my hands and I'll throw back my head
And I'll feel that sweet grace once again

Grace is bigger than our circumstances. Mons allowed me to exist in my truest self. I had a safe place to express joy and sorrow freely without shame. I had a community that recognized my strengths and encouraged me to walk in them. God can change everything in a moment, and that rainy January day was the moment He did so for me.

Today I sit here writing this in Trier, Germany, which we now call *home*, not knowing what the future holds. I cling tightly to the truth of my miracle in Mons. God knows me best, and He will always lead me towards my true identity. The more I surrender, the less fear can take hold. And the more I surrender, the more I experience true grace. It can be messy, it can be painful, it can be confusing. But surrendering to the truth that you are where you are meant to be is incredibly freeing. My true home is eternal.

According to French philosopher and paleontologist Pierre Teilhard de Chardin, we are not human beings having a spiritual experience; we are spiritual beings having a human experience. Home is under the shadow of God's wings. Guided by grace, we are safe.

REST AND REFLECTION

Your Name

Take a moment to sit and ponder with Jesus.

By now as you've been reading our stories, you've likely been reminded of your own situation or pain.

He wants to heal you, He wants to restore you.

As you quiet your heart, invite Jesus into that memory.

Ask Him where He was.

Ask Him to show you how He is healing you right now.

As He pours His restoration in, journal what that looks like.

Is He showing you a picture?

Giving you a verse?

Maybe He is whispering words into your spirit.

A LAMENT

Connie Lucille Peachey

Grief and sorrow are an inevitable part of living. On this side of heaven life gets hard and we often struggle to make sense of our pain. In our culture, it is often not acceptable to be in mourning for any significant length of time. It is uncomfortable to sit with the grieving, to hear them process their pain out loud over and over. So, we bury our pain and suffer alone in silence. We do not know how to lament.

A lament is giving voice to our struggle with grief, loss, trauma, pain, terror, sorrow, etc. It is stating that we are not okay with the way things are. Most often, a lament will take us on a journey toward recognizing God as the Almighty who will intervene and, therefore, is worthy of our praise. I'm not sure we can effectively praise God without first acknowledging our pain.

I wrote this lament during a six-month leave of absence from our ministry. The pain of my past was no longer willing to take a silent back seat. I had to face it head on and work my way through the darkness to the light.

O LORD, have mercy. You are my only hope.
My distress is such that my joints cry out in pain;
My muscles clench in spasm.
My heart is crushed.
Is there to be no end to this pain and sorrow?

Just when I finally have enough strength to stand
My enemy knocks my feet out from under me.
Again. And. Again.
I am all alone; my tears pour down like rain.
I have tried to walk this journey in my own strength;
With my own wisdom.
I am naked before You, LORD.
I have nothing to add to Your grace.
I remember You have kept me close to Your heart;
You never let me stray far away from You.
Even when it is so dark I cannot see my hand in front of my face
You, O LORD, lead me with Your Right Hand.
You go before me.
Your angels stand as my guardians against the enemy.
You and You alone can give the order to rescue me from my distress.
Please come to my aid.
Please rescue me from destruction.
Without Your intervention I will surely perish.
Stretch out the Strong Arm of the LORD
And lift me from this pit.
You are my God.
You are my only hope.
Because You are here I am NOT ALONE!
Nov 19, 2010

Inspired by: Ps 3:3; 4:1–3; 6:6–7; Isa 51:7–8, 12–16, 22 (NLT).

JOY FOR OTHERS

Deborah Carpenter

The day I knew for sure we were losing our home was just like any other day. A knock came on the door. It was a management company sent by the bank.

Our family had lost so much already and, despite all we had done to ensure the loss of the house would not happen, it seemed God was taking that too. I had worked so hard in the months following Andrew's accident to keep my joy. Losing our home seemed like one loss too many.

I told God how I felt about all of this and He responded gracefully as He always seems to. He reminded me of how He had faithfully provided for us in the past year since the accident. Then, He proved Himself faithful once again by providing a home for us to move into a few months later.

I was fighting for joy and thought I was winning the war. As I set up house in our new home, I was struck by how wonderfully gracious God had been to me despite my frustration with Him. That is, until one afternoon, when I logged into Facebook.

There, a very dear friend had posted pictures of her new home. As I sat in the basement of my very old rental property that smelled a little like mildew, I could not share her joy. Somewhere deep down I wanted to be happy for her and post a reply that joined her in her praise of a good God, but I just couldn't.

Over the next few hours, I struggled. Why not me? Why did God take my home? I focused on all my family had lost in the past year and I struggled to gain perspective. The joy I had fought so hard for was now just gone.

I was disappointed with myself. But perhaps I was a little more disappointed with God. And even though we weren't destitute, even though we had money to pay the rent and put food on the table, even though we had clothes to wear and Andrew was healing, I just couldn't be happy for my friend. Losing our house overshadowed my joy for her in her new home.

I recalled Philippians 4:11–12 (ESV):

"Not that I am speaking of being in need, for I have learned in whatever situation I am to be content. I know how to be brought low, and I know how to abound. In any and every circumstance, I have learned the secret of facing plenty and hunger, abundance and need."

As I pondered this verse, I realized that I was very good at being content while abounding in plenty. I thought I was good at being brought low, as I had endured a year of it after Andrew's accident. Even losing the house was a low that I thought I was content with—until someone else gained what I had lost.

My problem was my perspective. I went back to Philippians 4 and read what Paul had written a few verses earlier.

"Finally, brothers, whatever is true, whatever is honorable, whatever is just, whatever is pure, whatever is lovely, whatever is commendable, if there is any excellence, if there is anything worthy of praise, think about these things. What you have learned and received and heard and seen in me—practice these things, and the God of peace will be with you" (4:8–9).

My joy and contentment were predicated on my ability to "think on these things." When my eyes looked away from the good things God had already blessed me with and onto the things I thought God should have blessed me with, my joy and contentment vanished. In doing so, my peace vanished as well—and God felt far from me.

These verses tell us to "practice these things," which implies that this is not a natural response to life. It certainly seemed more natural to mourn what had been and focus on what was not. But if I wanted to be content and I wanted my joy—if I truly wanted the God of peace to be at work in my life—I need to practise thinking on these things.

While I was focusing on the material, God was considering the eternal.

Really, it wasn't about the house. It was about my heart, and God was revealing to me sin that needed to be brought to the cross. He wanted me to be content in Him. He wanted me to give up my demands about what a perfect life and outcome looked like. He didn't want to wrench it from my grip. He wanted me to give it to Him with perfect faith and trust. I couldn't do that without being able to "think on these things" first.

I believe that the reminder to "think on these things" was not only meant for my peace but was also meant to give me the perspective needed to love and encourage others truly and faithfully to "think on these things" as well. For so many of us, life has handed us pain and heartache—situations that defy the heart's ability to see the joy that is still to be had in life and to view God as the giver and perfecter of that joy. These situations can rob us of the ability to rejoice with those who rejoice. But God has given us the solution: "Think on these things."

A few days later, I logged back onto Facebook and posted a reply. I think it just said "I love it! What a blessing!" It wasn't much. But it was true.

COVERED

Brenda Goudy

"Whoever dwells in the shelter of the Most High will rest in the shadow of the Almighty. I will say of the LORD, 'He is my refuge and my fortress, my God, in whom I trust.' Surely he will save you from the fowler's snare and from the deadly pestilence. He will cover you with his feathers, and under his wings you will find refuge; his faithfulness will be your shield and rampart. You will not fear the terror of night, nor the arrow that flies by day" (Ps 91:1–5).

Raising three boys was no easy feat, but it was much sweeter by going through the joys and struggles alongside friends who helped share the load. I couldn't imagine getting through my days as a young mom without my other young mom friends, of which there were many. One such friend and I got along from the day we met, which was at church shortly after my husband and I moved to Calgary with our first son. We hit it off right away and quickly developed a fun and trusting friendship that continues to this day.

She is the kind of friend to whom I could admit my weird idiosyncrasies and, more often than not, discover that she had the same ones! That we like our iced tea hot sometimes, or bite our cuticles, or prefer plain chips over any other flavour is not knowledge you entrust to just anyone!

Years ago, when either of our husbands were travelling, we would find that our houses made strange noises in the night. We came up with a brilliant strategy to live through the fear this inevitably caused.

We would call the other person and leave the phones at our bedsides all night. That way, if one of us would ever scream we were sure it would wake the other up. Then they could call 911 and all would be well. This was, of course, in the days of home phone landlines, so our phones would be 'off the hook' all night. While rationally our solution didn't make a lot of sense, our fearful minds were eased knowing that the other person was there and, thankfully, both of us could sleep.

At the beginning of my separation, I found it very hard to sleep when my boys were at their dad's house. The creaks and noises seemed deafening, and they also played into my ongoing fear of possible danger at the hands of my ex-husband. By this time my friend had moved overseas with her husband, and having a long-distance all-night phone call was not an option. One night, when sleep was elusive and fear was strong, I knew that going to my Bible had to be the place to start. But where to read?

Since I was a little girl my dad had told me that if I didn't know where to read, just open the Bible and see where it lands. So that's what I did. My Bible opened to Psalm 91, and I stopped short at the words "You will not fear the terror of the night." I claimed that phrase then and there and memorized the verses written above. I have recited them to myself many times over the years, sometimes saying them out loud when the noises seem too real and strange. It never fails to ease my mind as I remember that I am safe with my Father. My security—my safety—is found in Him; I live in His shelter and shadow. He is my refuge and my fortress. I trust in Him.

I have not met anyone yet who has not experienced fear in some way. Life is full of fearful situations; some are "terrors of the night" and some are "arrows in the day." I encourage everyone to memorize these short verses and recite them whenever fear creeps in.

Our Father is standing over you with His wings surrounding you, protecting and loving you through all the fears you will ever encounter. I have lived this and known it to be true. His phone is always 'off the hook'; He is waiting to hear us call out to Him.

IDENTITY CRISIS

Lynda Blazina

Recently, as I was walking through a tough season, I found myself reading through one of my favourite stories in Scripture—the story of Joseph. On a Sunday not long after, I went to church with my daughter and her pastor was also speaking on Joseph. He made a statement in his sermon that radically changed my outlook on my circumstances. He said that "when Joseph's brothers stripped him of his coat he was, in part, stripped of his identity as well."

This made me take another look at Joseph's story.

Jacob had given the coat to Joseph to identify him as the oldest son of his favourite wife, the son for whom he had a deep love and affection. The coat had been constructed to stand out and to make Joseph stand out. It wasn't a regular shepherding coat. It wasn't made for labour.

The coat accomplished all that Jacob had wanted it to, even if the response wasn't in Joseph's favour! Not only did the coat create roots of envy and jealousy in Joseph's brothers, it became even more aggravating to them when Joseph began to receive dreams from the Lord. What did Joseph do? He searched out his brothers, who had been given plain shepherding coats, and let them know that he was something special. The coat had accomplished everything that Joseph had wanted it to as well (insert long sigh… *Oh, Joseph!*).

But then, in a fit of rage, his brothers took his coat, and with it everything that both he and Jacob had wanted it to identify in Joseph's life.

After the incident with the coat, Joseph's identity was no longer as Jacob's favourite son. Everyone in his life either believed or acted like he was dead. He was no longer known as special or set apart or favoured. He was just a slave boy. He was no longer the future ruler of his dreams. How could he possibly rule over anyone when he was living as a slave in a foreign country?

I then took another look at my story. How many of the 'coats' that had identified me had been stripped away in the past years? Many of the things I had believed about myself, and the titles I had been given or adopted as my own, now lay torn and bloodied at the bottom of some pit dug by nasty circumstances.

Because of the loss of my mom and dad, I was no longer a daughter to anyone on this earth. Family relationships had shifted and changed. I no longer pictured myself as the stellar mom or wife that I had once thought I was. I hadn't been able to protect or guide my kids through the trials they had faced. Ministry had taken a back seat to dealing with pain, suffering, and realities that I would have rather not found myself in. It didn't feel like I was blessed or favoured in God's sight anymore.

But…we have the advantage of taking another look at the whole story…

We know, because we can read the rest of the story, that Joseph was actually right where God wanted him to be. The identity that He had placed on Joseph was secure in His divine plan. Through all the trials Joseph endured, God reshaped the identity that Joseph had assumed and been given by others, in order to fulfill his God-given identity. One that he had, quite literally, dreamed of.

In our lives, when we face situations that don't seem to fit into the plan that God has revealed or the dreams that He has given us for our lives, we can always trust God. God is able to take everything that was "intended for evil"—every pain-filled moment—and use it for good. If God is able to use a murder plot, deception, slavery, an adulterous-minded woman, and imprisonment to ultimately bring about His purposes in Joseph's life, there is no limit to what He can use in our lives to bring His plans to fruition.

TRIGGER LANE

Charleen Raschke

Trigger: "anything, as an act or event, that serves as a stimulus and initiates or precipitates a reaction or series of reactions" (Dictionary.com, Oct 2018).

Triggers happen to us regularly. A trigger could be a smell, a sound, a sight or the way someone says something. Something happens to send us off into a memory, either positive or negative.

I was in grade school in the seventies. I lived in a small community, where our only school went from kindergarten to grade 12. The bullying began all the way back in grade one and it followed me through to grade 10.

I was an athletic child, good at sports such as track and field, baseball and volleyball. I remember clearly running a 200-yard dash and leaving most of my classmates in the dust. I loved running in races, and I loved the feeling of winning because I worked hard to win.

In many gym classes, the teacher would choose two captains, who would then take turns choosing their teams. And even though I was better than several of the other students in physical ability, it never failed. I was typically chosen last.

This was a bullying tactic, and it affected me deeply. But it went on for so many years that I came to expect it, all the while being very aware that I deserved better than I was receiving. I grew up watching others, less deserving, getting recognition that should have been mine.

When you work really hard for something and then watch someone else get rewarded in your place, it eats away at your desire to even want to try. Why bother? What's the point?

As an adult, I have worked through much of my past, but I often wonder if I will ever be finished working through it on this side of heaven. Will I ever find complete healing? While we can be healed from damage done to us as children, such healing requires surrender, forgiveness and not giving up. Because of the damage done to me as a child, I continued to choose poorly in the friend department well into my adult life. I desperately wanted bullies to like me.

Several years ago, I organized a party to celebrate a family member's birthday. Some of the conversations that took place among the people I had gathered to celebrate with us caused our adult children to feel uncomfortable. So a few days after the party, my daughter had a heart-to-heart conversation with me. It was her insight that caused me to take a look at some of my friend choices from a new perspective. She asked me why I had chosen bullies to be my friends over the years.

Her question was like a spotlight shining on an issue I didn't even know existed. This was the moment where I had a choice to make. I could either shrug it off *or* I could decide to take a deeper, more honest look at what the problem might be.

Thankfully I chose the latter. She was right! I needed this broken piece healed by Jesus. I needed to work through the issue, and I would need to place some boundaries around my heart. I contacted a trusted friend and arranged for some extended prayer ministry directly connected to this issue.

Proverbs 4:23 says:

"So above all, guard the affections of your heart, for they affect all that you are. Pay attention to the welfare of your innermost being, for from there flows the wellspring of life" (TPT).

There was one more piece of healing that I kept hearing Jesus whisper to my heart. He told me to trust Him to bring the right people into my life. I didn't need to try to make it happen. He would do it for me.

Today I am still aware of moments when I know I deserve something I have worked hard for, but have not received. It doesn't happen as often as it once did, but I can still experience triggers like anyone else. The triggers take me right back to grade school. The same feelings arise; the same insecurities.

I have come to recognize that obviously life is not fair, and that I don't have to stay wallowing in my own self-pity. I have learned to challenge myself with "Can I be happy for the person who got what should have been mine?" It's when I can honestly answer "Yes" that I realize I am freer, and that the past junk no longer has its hold on me.

— DAY 20 —

EXILED

Kerry Robideau

"I know what I'm doing. I have it all planned out—plans to take care of you, not abandon you, plans to give you the future you hope for" (Jer 29:11, MSG).

Exiled! That's not a word we use a lot in North America. People are exiled from countries, or exiled to prison, but have you ever thought of being spiritually or emotionally exiled?

If I think back over the last 15 years of my life, I can see many areas and ways in which I was exiled. With the exile came loss—loss of family, loss of my church family, loss of job, loss of my home and community that I loved, loss of dreams, hope and future, leaving me in a state of discouragement and, at times, despair. I wondered where my God of miracles was and why He would leave me and my family in this state of being.

Back in 2004, we were forced to move away from our home, our church family, and the community that we had come to love. A series of events took place within the church we were pastoring that wouldn't allow us to stay, due to irreconcilable differences and betrayal. We were willing to work out the differences but the other party was not. At the same time, my father-in-law had just come out of the hospital after four months of waiting for a heart transplant, and we found out that my mother was diagnosed with stage three ovarian cancer, which ended up being terminal. It was an overwhelming and difficult time in our lives.

My husband and I and our three sons were all affected. Our oldest two were in junior high and high school. They were at a tough age to be moving away from their friends, and they were unsure of how to handle what was happening with my mom. My husband and I were a mess! Devastated and beaten, we didn't feel like we had much to offer our children in the way of parenting and support with our own sense of guilt piled on top of everything else. I'm sure they felt as lost as we did.

Exiled! Emotionally, physically, and spiritually sent into exile from the people and community we loved, into a place of wilderness, a territory unknown to us.

Most Christians have Jeremiah 29:11 memorized or have used it to claim God's goodness in their lives at some point. I have done the same, but recently Jesus asked that I take a deeper look at this Scripture. Then He gave it to me as a promise for the near future.

The nation of Israel was taken captive and exiled to Babylon when Jeremiah was prophet. God spoke through him to deliver His message of hope and dreams for His people in their time of loss. God's Word reads:

"I'll show up and take care of you as I promised and bring you back home" (29:10). "When you come looking for me, you will find me. When you get serious about finding me and want it more than anything else, I'll make sure you won't be disappointed" (29:12–13). "I'll turn things around for you. I'll bring you back from all the countries into which I drove you—God's decree—bring you home to the place from which I sent you off into exile. You can count on it" (29:14, MSG).

Sometimes God's timing is so hard to understand. The Israelites had to wait for seventy years to see His promise come true. It can feel that long when we are in the midst of our own exile experiences, but even in the middle of those experiences God wants to bless and see increase in our lives.

In verses 5–8, God tells Israel to keep increasing even in exile, to plant gardens, build houses, to marry and have children, to make a home and work for the country's welfare, and (this is the hard one) to pray for the land they were exiled to, because if the land has peace and prosperity, so will they.

I can attest to that. In the midst of our own exile experience, God provided finances when we had no jobs. He provided a home to cover our heads, and friends and family to help carry the load when it was too overwhelming for us to bear by ourselves.

Fifteen years… Wow! It's been a rollercoaster ride for sure with its ups and downs and round and round, wondering if we were ever going to get off this ride, but God is faithful. His promises are true. I can't say that we have 'arrived' or that we are out of the woods totally, but we are seeing God's blessing in our futures, in our children's lives, and, the best part, an increase in our relationship with Jesus. The deadness we felt for so many years is lifting, and hope is filling its place.

Babylon was defeated, and the Israelites were freed to return home with full blessing. My 'Babylon' was defeated, and I was freed to return to my 'home'—not physically back to the home from which we came, but to the home of emotional and spiritual freedom. On this side of the exile there is peace, blessing, and the returning of what was lost. We have experienced increase in family, good jobs, a home, a return of ministry opportunities, and blessing in business.

I encourage you to be patient for God's timing for your freedom. He knows your day of salvation but in the waiting be fruitful and multiply, bless those who curse you, forgive, seek Him with all your heart, cry out to Him. He hears you, He has you in His arms taking care of you, and He has a plan for you.

REST AND REFLECTION

Your Name

If you were asked how your relationship with the Holy Spirit is, how would you answer?

Sometimes, even when we've walked in faith for a long time, our relationship with God seems dry or disconnected from our real life.

Often this is because we are not communicating with the Holy Spirit.

Take a moment to ask the Holy Spirit to reveal Himself to you, then read 1 Corinthians 3 to 5.

What is He telling you through this Scripture?

Based on what you believe He revealed to you, journal your response to Him.

If you have been reading through Scripture daily, continue on your plan, journalling what the Holy Spirit reveals to you each day, and your response to Him.

BATTLE PREP

Lisa Clarke

I remember the night I could hear water running for what seemed like hours. My oldest daughter had gone into the shower and had evidently curled herself up in a ball and lain there, feeling the hot water fall on her body.

She had been quiet at supper and somewhat distant. I could tell she was in mental anguish as I watched her across the table. Her brow was furrowed and she looked distraught. But as I asked her about her day she just blankly stared down at her plate and responded with a slow "Fine." I hate the word *fine*. It tells me nothing. It just ends a conversation. But that moment wasn't the right time to probe or press her. So I abandoned the hope of finding out why my girl was in so much distress.

As I walked down the basement stairs, steam was starting to creep out from under the bathroom door. I gently knocked and felt the warm air around my feet. "Jess," I called. "Jess, honey, open the door."

Ever since her 14th birthday I had begun to see some changes in her personality. The most apparent change was her outward demeanour. A sadness had taken over her, gripped her, and was holding her hostage. Again, "Jess, open the door, honey." A little sound, almost like a moan, answered back. "Go away, I need to be alone."

In my head I thought, "That's a lie Satan is feeding you." But I realized it probably wasn't a good idea to point that out, so I began to pray. Well, that is not the entire truth. I had been praying at dinner, as I walked downstairs, and as I stood in front of the bathroom door. These days I felt like I lived in a continuous place of prayer. Not knowing what to do, not knowing how to help my family, and, on this given day, not knowing how to help my precious daughter.

"Jess. Please, honey, open the door." This time I heard the shower curtain pull back and her footsteps coming towards me. She unlatched the door. As the steam enveloped us, she crawled back into the tub and let the warm water fall on her frail body again. I sat on the edge of the tub trying to console her. She had been crying for over an hour. Her eyes where red and swollen, possibly from the combination of salty tears and hot water splashing her face.

"My love," I said, "What is it? What is it you're battling right now? I can tell you are carrying so much. Let me help you. Tell me what you're thinking."

She let me wrap her in a towel and I held her for a long time. Then she told me how much she was struggling with some boys in her class.

The problem was so much bigger than she even let on. At the time, I thought it was normal teenage angst. However, as months played out, a darkness and evil would be exposed. It would take me back to my own young years and remind me of pain I wasn't really prepared to face.

I tucked her into bed that night, prayed over her, and watched her as she succumbed to a deep sleep. As I walked out of her room and closed the door I was again brought back to a time in my past when I was in despair, feeling alone, confused, and extremely vulnerable.

I was feeling a desperation for my daughter, not knowing where the months ahead of us would lead. The writer of Proverbs exhorts readers to "Trust in the LORD with all your heart and lean not on your own understanding. In all your ways acknowledge him and he will lead your path" (Prov 3:5–6).

So why was I so wobbly? Why was I feeling so unsettled, almost tipsy?

Waves crashed against rock in my mind that night, and I began to feel very ill—unable to catch my own breath.

As I drifted off to sleep, I thought of Ephesians 1:18–20:

"I pray that the eyes of your heart may be enlightened in order that you may know the hope to which he has called you, the riches of his glorious inheritance in his holy people, and his incomparably great power for us who believe. That power is the same as the mighty strength he exerted when he raised Christ from the dead and seated him at his right hand in the heavenly realms."

Even in those drowsy moments of falling asleep, God was equipping me to be ready for the battle ahead.

Things got much worse before they got better. I'm glad we can't see ahead. We think we would be okay if we just knew what was coming. However God, in His mercy, is with us regardless of our circumstances.

My focus that night with Jess was not on the one who saved me, Jesus. Could you blame me? But I know that's not the point. The point is that my Saviour, who knew the future, was going before her and me. He was preparing our steps; preparing my heart and mind.

He was bringing His Word to mind, reminding me of situations in my past that I could draw on to help my daughter; reminding me of those situations I still needed healing from. Preparation didn't make the battle easy, but it did let me know that He was *with* me in it all.

LOSING CONTROL

Connie Lucille Peachey

2006 began like a normal year. There were no warning signs that my life was about to be turned upside down. My MO and identity as a 'control freak' was about to come to a halt. I used to think that being a control freak was actually a strength, and I would introduce myself as such with a sick sense of pride. I reared my children under this tyranny and often insisted they do things my way because I knew it was the best and most efficient way to get a job done (hint: sarcasm). There was not a lot of wiggle room and the only acceptable response to a request I made was, "Yes, Mommy." I had very well-behaved children, at least on the outside. I used whatever method I could to manage my household and get people to do what I wanted them to do, how I wanted them to do it.

In February 2006, my 'normal' exploded with a series of events beyond my control. We were just over a year into a brand-new pastoral ministry when our 17-year-old daughter and her boyfriend sat us down and told us she was pregnant. They were in grade 12 with a bright future ahead of them.

I couldn't fix this. I had not planned for this. This was not how things were supposed to go. This was not the dream I had for my little girl, or for myself for that matter.

I was plunged into months of darkness. All my life I had read my Bible, prayed regularly, and had a sense of God's presence carrying me through life. All of a sudden I found myself in a free fall. This happened to other people. When it did, I had all kinds of wise words of grace for them. Now it was happening to me and the words sounded hollow in my soul. People told me, "Be sure you journal this journey. One day you will need to go back and read it."

So I did. I know that it was a difficult year, but as I reread my journals now, 11 years later, I realize that I had forgotten just how dark it was. For months there is no entry of hope in my journal. No recorded Bible reading, or food for my soul. There is just a pouring out of pain, sorrow, bitterness, anger, resentment, grief… This yoke was not easy, nor was it light.

In a three-month span my daughter graduated from high school seven months pregnant, my younger daughter graduated from grade nine, she and I went to Cuba on a mission trip (my older daughter had to cancel because of her pregnancy), my father passed away, the transmission on our van blew in the middle of hot, dry Saskatchewan on our way back to Alberta from my father's funeral in Manitoba (a nightmare I feared every time I crossed that wilderness), and my older daughter got married. *There was no time for God in all of this!* I was totally overwhelmed. Oh, and my son broke up with his girlfriend, the one we had thought was 'the one'; he moved home from college and brought a friend home for the summer, so in all of this we had a stranger living with us in our home.

When life gets crazy, my tendency is to try to make sense of things, to make things better, to hold everyone else up, to stand in the gap and be whatever is needed to hold the family together. If I don't, who will? This yoke was not easy, and the burden was not light.

Journal entry – May 8, 2006

I have been losing strength. When Cori and Riley first told us about the baby I said, "I don't want to waste this pain. I want to grow. I want to be able to use my story to help others. I want my story to point to Christ and how He makes beauty out of ashes." I feel like an ash heap.

Yesterday Tom preached about the Sabbath. Jesus Christ desires to be my Sabbath Rest. I have been screaming out for rest. All the while Christ has been saying, "Take My yoke upon you. Come to Me and I will give you rest. Connie, you are wearing yourself out trying to carry not only your yoke but the yoke of others. You were not meant to carry anyone else's yoke. Come here, slip your head into My yoke. My yoke is easy, My burden is light. Come, sweetheart, learn from Me. I will protect you. I will defend you if you stay with Me in My yoke."

Thus began my journey back to Jesus. I'd like to say the control freak left me for good that day, but it has been a slow process of relinquish–grab it back–relinquish–grab it back. But I have gained so much freedom. The beautiful thing is that Jesus never gave up on me. He never said, "Okay, that's it. I'm done. You are too stubborn!" He just keeps inviting me to switch out my yoke for His.

2006 was a battle for my soul. God had long allowed me to operate in partnership with a spirit of control. It was now time to let it go. God loves me too much to let things slide for too long. The choices of others were no longer under my influence or power to change. Life took a new trajectory—one I would never have chosen. But when I was able to lay down the yokes I was carrying for others, I made room in my soul for God to bring beauty where there had been despair and darkness. The road was not easy, but it rarely is when we have made friends with sinful patterns. God was inviting me to say goodbye to my way-too-familiar MO and take on His yoke, His burden, and to hand control of my life and future over to Him; to trade all these extra yokes for His one yoke. He always trades up, my friends!

The temptation to control still crouches at the door of my soul, and from time to time I make agreements with it and allow it to influence my life. I am growing in my ability to recognize it for what it is, to renounce it in the name of Jesus, and to move into trusting God with my future and with those around me, even when their choices have ramifications for my life.

In Matthew 11, Jesus said:

"Come to me, all of you who are weary and carry heavy burdens, and I will give you rest. Take my yoke upon you. Let me teach you, because I am humble and gentle, and you will find rest for your souls. For my yoke fits perfectly, and the burden I give you is light" (Matt 11:28–30, NLT).

"Come to Me. Learn from Me. Rest in Me." — Jesus

P.S. I have the most amazing grandson ever! And the Lord has blessed me with two more since then. He has brought so much beauty out of such a difficult path. God is good.

HIS THORN, MY THORN

Charleen Raschke

The day started out normal enough. My husband left the house early so that he could prepare for church and then later help lead our congregation in worship. This made my morning a little more interesting, with a little more work, as normally my husband gets our son ready on Sunday mornings, except on the days he volunteers in worship.

Our son is 26 years old now. He is a joy to our family in many, many ways, which is why going where I'm about to go is so hard. I don't want him to be viewed in a negative light in any way.

He has multiple disabilities, which affect our lives in multiple ways. I would never even attempt to compare what feels difficult for me with what is difficult for him every single day. There is no way those things can or should be compared, ever!

That being said, where I am wanting to go here is straight to my marriage. Caring for our adult son 24/7 has effects on our marriage.

I can honestly say that I feel very carried by God's grace *most* of the time, just as I did when he was a little guy. I really do! My son's care doesn't weigh on me negatively *most* of the time. But every now and then, it's almost as though the 'grace veil' gets lifted and I am allowed to *feel* what it would be like to not have grace present.

Back to yesterday. I got him ready and the two of us drove the 25 minutes to church. I got him out of the car and helped him into the sanctuary. We worshipped along with the people there. When the music ended, as usual, my husband helped him back to the foyer until the sermon was completed.

We joined in the after-church activity, then got in our vehicles and drove back home. I needed to stop for groceries, so I left to grab some things at our closest store and the farmer's market.

By the time I was unpacking the groceries at home, I wanted to do something different. It was a beautiful, sunshiny day and I wanted the three of us to get out and do something together. And this is where my day shifted—where the normal grace seemed to leave me.

My husband had been dreaming of walking along the river to fish (which means he goes alone, as our son cannot manage walking on those paths), and I was hoping we could spend time together. He left shortly after, while I was left to care for our son for the next several hours alone.

Many, many times, this kind of time alone with him is no big deal at all, it really isn't! But *this* day, I had a hope and a dream in my heart and there was nothing I could do to make it happen.

You could say I started to have a pity party, or you could say I allowed myself to feel the grief that crept into my heart. Grief over not going for a walk with my husband whenever I want to. Grief over not having a lot of freedom with my husband in many ways because of our situation. We will likely never be empty nesters; our son needs us. And there are moments when that takes its toll on me, on us.

I have felt these feelings before. They seem to come to the surface for me here and there, spread throughout the years. But I don't stay there. I don't really want to stay there. I allow myself to feel it, to grieve it, but then as I pray and worship, God once again breathes His grace back into my life.

I had tears. I had feelings that felt hurt. I felt trapped and I felt alone. Most of the people we know don't have to deal with this sort of thing, though a few do.

It's not easy. It is a sacrifice. But it is worth it. Our son is incredibly worth sacrificing for. It's what we are called to—to be that steady, stable constant in his life. And because of this, he knows he's loved and he feels safe.

In 2 Corinthians 12, Paul talks about having a "thorn in his flesh" that torments him. Three time he pleads with the Lord to remove it. The Lord replies, in verse 9, "My grace is sufficient for you, for my power is made perfect in weakness."

STEPPING INTO THE UNKNOWN

Deborah Carpenter

The ICU family room was filled with people. One doctor. He sat on the blue plastic chair and gave us Andrew's official diagnosis. Andrew had a severe traumatic brain injury complicated by fatty embolisms due to his multiple broken bones. He might never wake up from his five-day coma. Then again, he could wake up. If he did, it would not be a sprint to healing—it would be a marathon. The doctor said he wished it were better news, but all he had for us was a diagnosis with no known outcomes and no known treatments. Only time would tell.

There was stunned silence in the room. The doctor rose, and I followed him out of the room. I thanked him for his compassionate care of my husband. It was all I could thank him for. He nodded and said, "You're welcome." There was nothing more to say.

I returned to the family room and sat and listened to Andrew's other family members and friends. I can't say how they were feeling, but I kept hearing the words "unknown" over and over in my head. We had come together to hear from the doctor, and I think we had all been praying for a more hope-filled diagnosis. Someone spoke about how they knew God would heal him. I wasn't so sure. It wasn't that I didn't believe God could. I just didn't know if God would.

As family and friends made their way out of the room, making promises to continue to pray, offering me words of encouragement, and making declarations of God's ability and willingness to work a miracle, I sat in my own plastic chair and tried to take in what I had heard. I knew that my little family was at the starting gate of a race with no known finish line. In that moment, I realized we didn't need declarations or pronouncements of miraculous healing. We needed something to motivate us to take the first step into the unknown.

The unknown can be dark and foreboding. It gives space for the imagination to fill in the blanks with worst-case scenarios devoid of hope. As believers in a God who saves, I think we know better than to give our mind over to the darkness, but we aren't always sure where to look for the light. We need faith to believe that there is light, somewhere. So I prayed, feebly, "I believe. Please help my unbelief." And that was all I could pray.

A few days later I would get the call that my daughter had suffered a ruptured appendix. As we were all focused on Andrew, her condition, which we thought was the flu, went undiagnosed until she was just hours from death due to septic shock.

As we drove to the hospital where she was having surgery, I wasn't sure how things could get any darker. I was surprised that my heart was still beating. My lungs were still breathing, but my mind could not and would not pray. The faith I had prayed for seemed to be gone, like the inkling of a fragment of a dream. A few hours later, I stood in yet another family room trying to comprehend how I was going to be at a hospital in one city and a hospital in another city. I was absolutely undone.

Yet, that prayer had been prayed. And the beauty of that prayer is this: it acknowledged that my faith existed in some form or another. It might have only been a desperate desire for even a mustard seed-sized faith. But it called upon the author and perfecter of my non-existent faith to give me what I did not have and what I could not muster on my own: a faith that could move a mountain, even if that mountain had fallen on top of me and crushed my very spirit.

The power of that prayer is this: God heard. The promise of that prayer is this: God would answer with a resounding YES.

In the midst of the prayers and the encouraging words, the only reason I could step into the unknown that day was that I could step into it with the one who knew my greatest need. He knew I needed to give Him my unbelief.

In the middle of the dark unknown, there is only one who knows. He sees us and has not left us alone in the dark without a guide. He offers us His hand and promises to lead us through it. He may not make the path bright, but He will give us faith to take the next step. He gives it beside the hospital bed. He gives it at the graveside. He gives it in the lawyer's office and the courtroom. He gives it to the parent who is watching a wayward child flee farther and farther from the truth. He gives it to the one who has fallen into sin and wonders if forgiveness is even possible. He gives, and He gives, and He gives, to all who pray "I believe. Help me in my unbelief."

DO NOT FEAR

Lynda Blazina

If you read Scripture, it won't be long before you read a verse about fear. A couple of well-known verses are:

"So do not fear, for I am with you;
do not be dismayed, for I am your God.
I will strengthen you and help you;
I will uphold you with my righteous right hand" (Isa 41:10).

"For God has not given us a spirit of fear, but of power and of love and of a sound mind" (2 Tim 1:7).

"Therefore do not worry about tomorrow, for tomorrow will worry about itself. Each day has enough trouble of its own" (Matt 6:34).

"Do not be anxious about anything, but in everything, by prayer and petition, with thanksgiving, present your requests to God. And the peace of God, which transcends all understanding, will guard your hearts and minds in Christ Jesus" (Phil 4:6–7).

I heard someone once say that if we live with anxiety in our lives, it is because we are not taking the command "Do not fear" to heart, and therefore anxiety is an act of disobedience to God.

This caused me a great deal of anxiety! (See what I did there?)

If anxiety is sin, how do I simply change it to *not* sin? It's not like there is a tap or valve on me to shut off the emotion of fear or the out-flowing of anxiety when I find myself in situations of extreme distress or anxiety-inducing circumstances.

There have been many times in my life that I have felt extreme fear and anxiety, and yet I have always had a deep desire to follow Jesus. Not only that, but some of the times in my life during which I seemed to be riddled with fear were the times in my life that I also felt the closest to the Lord.

So, is "Do not fear" a command that I wasn't following, and was I therefore subject to live my days with unsettled anxiety? Was I living in a constant state of sin?

When you look at the Scriptures that talk about fear, I believe that you have to take what we know of God's character, and how He describes Himself, into account. God describes Himself as loving and compassionate and full of mercy and slow to anger. With these descriptions of Himself in mind, it is hard to imagine Him giving us a harsh military-type command of "Do not fear" with the expectation that we are sinning if we step out of line of the command.

God also calls Himself Father. As a parent, I know that some of the deepest sorrows and hurts that my children have walked through have come with a measure of fear attached: How will people react? How will I get past this? When will this be over? How will my life be affected?

I believe that, in Scripture, God tells us "Do not fear" with the same parental compassion in His voice that I want to convey to my kids when they come to me with burdens and cares.

I don't hear these word as 'commands' but as the gentle voice of my heavenly Father saying, "It's okay, honey. I know this is painful and you're worried, but know that I've got it in My hands. I know the outcome and I have the power to redeem it all. I hold the balance of the world and the trajectory of your soul in the palm of My hand. You don't have to carry this burden. There is no need to be anxious when I am your God."

When I focus on God's character and who He reveals Himself to be, it is much easier to cast my cares upon Him. "Do not fear" becomes a gentle beckoning toward a loving and compassionate Father, rather than a command from a gruff militant that I want to run from.

This is God's heart.

He longs for His children to love Him and to know that they are loved by Him.

Also, read the complete verse. God doesn't simply say "Do not fear." He tells us why: "For I am your God, for I am with you"; "I will strengthen and uphold you"; "You are mine." He essentially tells us throughout Scripture, "I've got this!"

The next time you hear or read "Do not fear," ask God to reveal *why* you don't have to fear. Ask Him to show you the reality of His character and who He is to you so that you are fully aware of how little you have to worry.

I guarantee you that He is sufficient to handle every trouble and trial that comes your way.

LIFE-GIVING BOUNDARIES

Stefanie Carlson

I have always known I was called to be a mother. I grew up babysitting young kids, and caring for special needs children through the summers when I was in high school. It came easily to me and I easily created bonds with those children. I have always been excited about the idea of my own children, and I couldn't wait to meet these little pieces of me.

I have been a mom for seven short years, and have only begun this journey of guiding my children and learning from them. But in my short years as a mother, I have also embarked on the amazing journey of owning a business. My business started very organically, just taking a few clients every month over my maternity leave, doing family members' or close friends' hair, and earning some side money. It was almost too easy! I could do hair while baby-wearing, and as my oldest daughter grew she was adored by all my clients.

From there, it just grew. I met and bonded instantly with an amazing, talented photographer, who encouraged me to build up my career to only having to work a few weekends per month. Every interaction I had in meeting new people fed my need to create and also contributed financially for my family! It fed me in every way, encouraging my social life and making those moments I had with my daughter even more precious.

My business continued to grow! After doing so many photo shoots I finally had a portfolio, and began to grow my wedding clientele. I even had regular hair clients in my home-based salon. My business organically grew alongside my business partner and her successes, and I came to a place where I needed more help. Two years in, I teamed up with another amazing friend and fellow hair/makeup artist, and our business was born. The opportunities that have come from this threesome partnership have surpassed any expectation that I ever had when I started working from home.

But everything has a season, and my season of work, travel, and grind has left me exhausted and afraid. I am left now with major mom guilt wondering if I have wasted the precious moments when my children were just forming into themselves as tiny humans. I have had a full-time, live-out nanny for the past four years, and the number one thing I respond to people when asked how I'm doing is "busy and tired." To the outside world, through social media, all you see is success, but in nearly every aspect of my life I feel guilt. I need boundaries.

I am a firm believer that our words have power, and I have been saying over myself that I'm busy and tired for years. Too tired to do that craft with my children. Too lazy to take my dog for a walk. Too busy to plan that lunch with girlfriends, or to have that date night with my husband. I started my business with the promise of day-to-day freedoms, of being present with my children and not missing moments because of my work schedule. Now I find myself working more than ever, and am left feeling completely drained.

I am in a season of shift, balance, and change, none of which are easy. I can sit and think about the things I have missed, not from just physically being away when I'm travelling for work but also from mentally being so spread out that I wasn't really present in any aspect. It leaves me to wonder what things would look like had I made different decisions. What if I had healthy boundaries? I don't regret being a working mom, and the relationships that I have built along the way are incredible. I'm in a shift season—shifting focus, priorities, and my own personal truths. However, I can't help but think of how things would be different if I had set up boundaries from the beginning.

I was recently talking to a friend and she asked this simple question: "What is the difference between water and steam?" I was thinking to myself… "That one is water and one is steam?" (Hilarious, right?) She responded, "One degree. The difference between water and steam is literally one degree. Give one percent more effort or attention and you will see transformation happen in your life." The opposite is also true. The difference between water and ice is also one degree. One degree less leaves a stagnant, still block of ice—hard and breakable. This thought left me with a new purpose, and I heard God speaking to me through this simple thought.

Romans 12:2 says:

"Do not conform to the pattern of this world, but be transformed by the renewing of your mind. Then you will be able to test and approve what God's will is—his good, pleasing and perfect will."

Even though I know I'm in a transition of time management and scheduling, my efforts will be for nothing if I don't give a bit more effort in each situation. This sounds backwards when I am trying to do less; however, anyone reading this could agree that one percent more effort is always possible.

No matter how busy and tired you are, especially if you have set boundaries that cannot be crossed, give one more degree of effort to the right things. If I set up proper time management boundaries in my business, my social life, my marriage and my family, I will be more than able to give a bit more without feeling guilty! I won't feel so worn down and spread so thin. I will have the energy to give that extra one percent and will feel recharged in the process.

REST AND REFLECTION

Your Name

"I lift up my eyes to the mountains—where does my help come from? My help comes from the LORD, the Maker of heaven and earth" (Ps 121:1–2).

In the midst of your journey, what was the point that you realized God was truly there for you?

If you haven't, what is holding you back from knowing this truth?

How did it change you, or how do you think it would change you to realize that God is there for you?

I CAN ONLY IMAGINE

Lisa Clarke

"I can only imagine…" When I think of these words from the song by MercyMe, I delight in the thought of my father. My heavenly Father, that is. I think of how it will make me feel to be worshipping our great God on the day I stand before Him.

The psalmist says:

"Restore us again, O God of our salvation, and put away your indignation towards us" (Ps 85:4, NRSV).

"Will you not revive us again that your people will rejoice in you?" (Ps 85:6).

I can imagine David dancing before the Lord—feeling free and lifted up. Then I turn the truth of these verses to myself and feel the same reckless abandon that David must have—delight in breathing God's love without end.

I cleaned out my wallet the other day, marvelling over the stuffed papers and utter clutter that made the pile before me. There were old receipts and tiny crumpled lists from months before. Full and heavy. I have often referred to the time I have spent on earth as a great weight— the wallet reminded me of the trappings of this world and the burdens we sometimes carry.

But then I was reminded that in Revelation 21:1–7 John paints an incredible picture—God is making all things new. There is a picture of a Holy City coming down from the heavens and this incredible new story comes bursting forth—no more tears, no more crying or mourning. "Death shall be no more" is trumpeted from the heavens.

I will rejoice on that day, the day I get to see my daughter again. I can imagine that I will dance and shout and leap and praise God. I will be in awe of the God who raised the dead and healed the lame and caused the blind to see. My earthly 'wallet' will be cleaned out and the weight of this world will be gone. I will live forever with my God.

Colossians 2:6–7 (ESV) says:

"Therefore, as you received Christ Jesus the Lord, so walk in Him; rooted and built up in Him and established in faith, just as you were taught, abounding in thanksgiving."

Also, Colossians 3:1–4 (ESV):

"If then you have been raised with Christ, seek the things that are above, where Christ is, seated at the right hand of God. Set your minds on things that are above, not on things that are on earth. For you have died, and your life is hidden with Christ in God. When Christ who is your life appears, then you also will appear with him in glory."

When I meditate on these verses, and recognize the glory of Jesus, I can set my mind on the things that are above, rather than the weight and heaviness of things here on earth.

My 'wallet' becomes a little lighter as I imagine the glory that Melissa is already experiencing and recognize the promise that I will get to share in that glory with her someday.

I can only imagine…

HOPE

Charleen Raschke

Hope
Hope like an anchor
Keeping me
Steadying even in the fiercest of storms
A life preserver
Hope holds my head above waters that threaten to drown
Hope seeds that need, nurturing and protecting
A tiny seed of light, defying darkness
Hope never gives up, ever
Hope says, "Hang on!"
Hope says, "Don't let go!"
Hope says, "Don't give up!"

We have all experienced some form of assault on our hearts at some point; maybe even at several points in our lives. Our souls have a very real enemy who is set on destroying us at every turn.

It is warfare. Warfare that seeks to destroy who we are created to be. Warfare that is aimed at wiping out our God-given hope.

Hope: "to look forward to with desire and reasonable confidence";
"to believe, desire, or trust"
(Dictionary.com, Nov 2018).

In the book of Hebrews, there is a connection between faith and hope:

"Now faith is the assurance (title deed, confirmation) of things hoped for (divinely guaranteed), and the evidence of things not seen (the conviction of their reality—faith comprehends as fact what cannot be experienced by the physical senses)" (Heb 11:1, AMP).

In the face of pain and tragedy, how does one hang onto hope? Is that even possible?

After a quick glance over my own life, I can say a confident "Yes." It is possible to hold on to hope. While the ways we each do this may be unique to us, there are likely some common threads when we take a deeper look.

As beings created in the image of God Himself, I believe it is in our DNA to hope. There is something hardwired in each of us that does not want to give up, even when things get thrown at us that scream "Give up, already!" We have something on the inside that wants to survive.

Even as a child, damaged as I was, I didn't want to give up. I *hoped* for my life to get better.

Several years later I met Hope Himself and my life *did get better*! As God restored my life piece by piece, I could see His love stamped on my life in so many ways all along the way.

Emotional healing and healthier relationships, along with a richer walk with Jesus, all contributed to a firm foundation deep within my identity of who I believe I am.

If you have been hurt, be assured that Jesus wants to heal your pain. He longs to free you from carrying it. You can trust Him. Will you give it to Him? Will you invite Him into that painful place so that He can bind up your wounds? He longs to meet you there.

— DAY 31 —

STICKS AND STONES

Brenda Goudy

"You intended to harm me, but God intended it all for good" (Gen 50:20, NLT).

"That is why we never give up. Though our bodies are dying, our spirits are being renewed day by day. For our present troubles are small and won't last very long. Yet they produce for us a glory that vastly outweighs them and will last forever!" (2 Cor 4:16–17, NLT).

The power of words cannot be underestimated. We all know that sticks and stones may break our bones but words will *always* harm us! And while we also know that our value comes from our identity in Christ, it is very difficult to ignore negative words that are spoken to us or over us, especially when they come from someone who should have our best interests in mind.

While in my marriage, I was continually put down, criticized and demeaned. I came to the point where I did not know what to believe. I struggled between believing the harsh and condemning words that were often spoken to me, and what I now know was the Holy Spirit, telling me that I was a valuable child of God just the way I was. He kept reminding me that He knew what was happening and that He hadn't forgotten me in the midst of it all.

One time, at a low point in my life, when I was told that my opinion was useless and no one would care what I had to say, God sent me a friend to challenge what I had been hearing.

At a critical point my friend said to me, "I've put your name in for the pastoral search committee at church because everyone I know values your opinion and wants to hear what you have to say."

God used the trust that this friend had in me to do a job within the church, to help me hear the positive opinions of others. He used someone outside my situation to reveal that I was seen as valued and wise. A woman of character within my Christian community.

"She speaks with wisdom, and faithful instruction is on her tongue" (Prov 31:26).

Another time, when I felt as if my appearance and my looks were being attacked and diminished, God again sent someone unexpected, and allowed me to hear His confirming and encouraging voice through a stranger.

As I was sitting in a restaurant, with my emotions raw and in distress, the young girl serving me said, "Excuse me, I'm sure you hear this all the time, but you are so beautiful, you look like Angelina Jolie."

Again, the Lord reversed the lies and hurtful words that I struggled with believing about myself, by sending someone to give me the opposite message of His truth. God sees us as His children, loves us abundantly and sees us as beautiful!

"I praise you because I am fearfully and wonderfully made; your works are wonderful, I know that full well" (Ps 139:14).

These are just two examples of the many times God showed up to refute lies that Satan would have loved for me to have believed.

This reminds me of the story of Joseph, whose brothers betrayed him, abused him, abandoned him, and sold him into slavery. The family that he should have been able to depend on to love and support him turned on him instead. Yet God used those actions for good. What humans mean for harm, God can miraculously change to bring about healing, hope and encouragement.

If you find yourself hearing words of hurt from people who are supposed to love and support you, don't be discouraged. It's so hard to protect your heart in the moment, but God is there and wants to change what is meant to hurt you into something good in your life. Watch for it, wait for it, and see how He will speak truth to you. And when it happens, share it! You never know who needs to hear it too.

ESCAPE ROUTE

Lynda Blazina

Anxiety: 1. "apprehensive uneasiness or nervousness usually over an impending or anticipated ill: a state of being anxious"

2. *medical*: "an abnormal and overwhelming sense of apprehension and fear often marked by physical signs (such as tension, sweating, and increased pulse rate), by doubt concerning the reality and nature of the threat, and by self-doubt about one's capacity to cope with it" (Merriam–Webster, Nov 2018).

All my life I've been known as a worry wart—someone who thought about life's 'what ifs' and worried unnecessarily about the improbable.

This may have stemmed from the childhood trauma of being attacked by a dog. I had been trying to flee to safety when I was attacked from behind. From that point on, l always felt the need to know of an escape route from any place where I felt like I could be trapped. If I could assess my situation, and know the best possible outcome should an attack of any sort happen, my chances of being injured would be lessened.

All of this was subconscious, of course.

It wasn't until years later, when one day I was verbalizing to my husband that I had an escape plan should thus and so happen, that I realized that this was not a normal thought process. A trauma had occurred at a point early enough in my development that it had changed the way I thought about life from that point forward.

The awareness of this fact allowed me to set aside the Houdini mindset for the most part and relax in situations where I knew that I was not in danger.

Recently, I realized that this mindset had snuck its way back into my outlook on life and become a source of anxiety to me. It startled me to realize that the same patterns of thinking that affected my actions in my physical life had also crept into my spiritual thinking.

I often viewed Satan as an attack dog, ready to devour me when I least expected it. I anticipated that he would cause great harm to me and the ones I loved unless I kept a constant eye open for him and had an escape route planned from every spiritually negative place I found myself in.

This mindset was subtly accentuated by parenting.

Often when my children found themselves in a situation that I deemed unsafe spiritually, I would voice my concerns in the form of "You should have…" or "You shouldn't have…" and tried desperately to hand my escape plans over to them.

One of my kids expressed to me the lack of trust they felt when I would voice such sentiments. They constantly felt like I was telling them that, no matter what they did, it wasn't good enough because it wasn't the way that I would have done it.

… And that was partly true.

My mothering instinct had overpowered my need to see them as smart, capable individuals in whom God was working. My protection of them ran roughshod over their independence.

While evaluating their critique of my actions, I realized something even further. In my need to feel safe, I wasn't trusting the one who is actually in control of their safety. Trying to implement *my* escape plans was hindering my ability to place my children into the loving hands of their heavenly Father.

As much as it is true that Satan may wish to devour us, God has provided the ultimate escape plan: Himself! It was only when I was able to turn my kids back over to the Lord, and trust in His great love for them, that I was finally able to rest. I could trust Him to always be the escape route, not just for me but for my kids as well.

"But the Lord is faithful, and he will strengthen you and protect you from the evil one" (2 Thess 3:3).

"Whoever dwells in the shelter of the Most High will rest in the shadow of the Almighty. I will say of the LORD, 'He is my refuge and my fortress, my God, in whom I trust.' Surely he will save you from the fowler's snare and from the deadly pestilence. He will cover you with his feathers, and under his wings you will find refuge; his faithfulness will be your shield and rampart" (Ps 91:1–4).

WHAT RIGHT DO YOU HAVE?

Kerry Robideau

"Therefore, as God's chosen people, holy and dearly loved, clothe yourselves with compassion, kindness, humility, gentleness and patience. Bear with each other and forgive one another if any of you has a grievance against someone. Forgive as the Lord forgave you. Over all these virtues put on love, which binds them all together in perfect unity" (Col 3:12–14).

But… But… But…

Oh, I sometimes wish I were an angel singing before Jesus, or warring for one of His children. Then I'd never get into trouble. It's really my reactions to other people's actions towards me that get me there. Not that I'm blaming them, but sometimes it just slips out before I realize what I've said.

Or it might be a belief that it's okay to hold on to my offence.

"But Lord, they wronged me. I have the right to hold on to my anger!"

"But Lord, they could wreck my life with what they just said!"

"But Lord, they are totally misunderstanding what I said, and twisting everything!"

"But Lord, they are going to get away with it and I'm the one left having to deal with the aftermath! It's not fair!"

As if my offence could change their behaviour.

I have had several people in my life who have misunderstood me and assumed conclusions against me and who I am. They then acted upon those conclusions by being angry with me, refusing to talk with me, or saying nasty things about me behind my back. I absolutely hate it when this happens and I know that my response stems from my own fears of what others think of me. I become fearful, offended, angry, and most often passive aggressive because it's just too scary to show my true emotions for fear that I will get beat up some more.

Then, in these situations, it somehow becomes my responsibility to have to make everything right. All the blame falls on me, and I'm supposed to grovel at their feet and ask for forgiveness! It truly isn't fair. I'm the innocent one and they get away with their wrongdoing because others around me don't want to get their hands messy and get involved.

Sound familiar?

There are two brothers in the book of Genesis named Jacob and Esau. They were twins. Esau, born first, became a hunter with hairy arms. Jacob, born second, was a tent-dweller with smooth arms. Because Esau was the oldest, he became the recipient of his father's death-bed blessing, as was the custom. Jacob, however, was a smooth man in more ways than one. While Esau was out hunting for his father, Jacob pretended to be Esau, feeding his father and receiving the father's blessing before Esau came back. Esau was devastated, and his offence was so great that he vowed to murder his brother (Gen 27:41).

I have to say that I would be devastated too if my brother stole from me. The Scripture says that Esau "bore a grudge." He held on to his offence and wasn't letting it go, to the point that he was willing to kill his brother!

Esau's sin was in how he responded to Jacob's deceit. I don't believe for one minute that Esau should have been okay with what Jacob did to him, but what should his response have been?

First, if our response to another's sin is less than godly, we need to repent. Yes! Acknowledge what you did wrong in complete humility and ask Jesus for forgiveness for your actions against your offender.

If you're like me, that will also mean anything done in secret, like harbouring the offence and carrying a nasty attitude toward the person. It may mean asking forgiveness for gossiping, lying, twisting the truth, cursing them, ignoring them, or some other form of subtle persecution. I didn't say it would be easy, and sometimes it takes time to let go of control and let God handle it for us. He does want to handle it for us.

What happens if you hold on to your grudge? 1 John 3:15 says: "Anyone who hates his brother is a murderer." Anger leads to bitterness which leads to hatred and, in Esau's case, even a willingness to murder his brother! If nothing else, our hearts grow cold and hard and the ability to love, grow, flourish, and enjoy life and God die with them. It's really not worth it.

The apostle Paul said: "I also do my best to maintain always a blameless conscience both before God and men" (Acts 24:16, NAS). While this verse doesn't mention it explicitly, we are safe to assume that Paul kept short accounts. He didn't let another's actions hold his emotions hostage; he repented of his own actions and he forgave.

Can you trust Jesus with your offenders? Can you acknowledge how your actions have been sinful and confess them and then forgive those who wronged you? It's the only way to freedom. If you can reconcile with them that's the best scenario, but if not (because it's not always possible—I certainly have a couple of situations myself where the other party isn't willing), still keeping your heart clean and free before God is the right thing to do. God will rule in perfect justice and perfect love. He wants your focus on Him. He wants you free to love Him and to love others.

Corrie ten Boom, who spent years in the brutal Nazi prison camps but loved Jesus, once said:

"Forgiveness is the key that unlocks the door of resentment and the handcuffs of hatred. It is a power that breaks the chains of bitterness and the shackles of selfishness" (*Clippings from My Notebook*).

It's time to let go!

— DAY 34 —

ABUNDANCE

Ryshon Blazina

"The good person out of the good treasure of his heart produces good, and the evil person out of his evil treasure produces evil, for out of the abundance of the heart his mouth speaks" (Luke 6:45, ESV).

Things in life come up all the time that shake us up. Maybe you see it coming, maybe you don't. Whether it is a breakup, a hurtful word, death, loss, anxiety, depression, or a hurting child, all these things have the power to shake us.

When we are shaken, whatever we have stored in our hearts gets spilled out. If you have been storing bitterness and anger and hurt in your heart, and been putting on a good face when life shakes you, you can bet that the bitterness and anger and hurt will eventually come out. In the same way, if you have kept a heart of peace and love and joy, that is what will come out when things don't go your way.

What is your speech saying about the condition of your heart today?

I love that this passage says it is out of the *abundance* of the heart that the mouth speaks. If you gather enough food for only yourself, odds are that you are going to eat it all. However, if you gather an abundance of food, you would want to and be able to share it with those around you.

The same goes for your heart and your time with Jesus. If you have an abundance of His presence and joy in your life, it will be impossible not to share it with those around you.

REST AND REFLECTION

Your Name

What is an area of abundance in your life?

Are there areas where you see this abundance spilling over into other people's lives?

WHEN GOD IS SILENT

Connie Lucille Peachey

"Even though the fig trees have no blossoms, and there are no grapes on the vines; even though the olive crop fails, and the fields lie empty and barren; even though the flocks die in the fields, and the cattle barns are empty, yet I will rejoice in the LORD! I will be joyful in the God of my salvation!" (Hab 3:17–18, NLT).

This picture looks bleak and silent, eerie and desolate. Where is God? The prophet opens the book with a question for God: "How long, O LORD, must I call for help, but you do not listen?"

When we read the stories of men and women of faith from the Scriptures, *we* see the whole picture. We see God intervening in miraculous and powerful ways. But let's take a walk in their shoes. Many of them waited a long time, through many years of seeming utter silence on the Lord's part, for resolution to their situations. Even when God was silent, they continued to trust Him.

Take Elijah. God told him it would not rain for three and a half years. Not only did it not rain, but we have no record of God saying any further words to Elijah as he waited out those years.

We read about Abraham and Sarah. They waited 25 years for their miracle baby to be born. Sarah had been barren all her life and was now well past childbearing. Yet God promised Abraham that he would have descendants as numerous as the stars by his wife Sarah. Then nothing. For 25 years, not a word.

Then there is Joseph. He was the favourite son of his father Jacob. God had given Joseph several dreams which revealed that he would one day be ruler over his brothers, and even over his parents. Before the dreams were ever realized he was sold as a slave to a far-off country. Just when he began to find favour in the eyes of his owner, the tables turned and he found himself unjustly imprisoned with no one to plead his case. His present reality was nothing like the dreams God had given him.

These people kept trusting God even in the bleakest of circumstances; even when God remained silent for years. I'm sure each of them in turn asked, "How long, O LORD, must I call for help, but you do not listen?" Or, "Are you even there, God?"

Many years ago, when my husband was in seminary, I had an opportunity to trust God even when He was not answering my prayers. We were at the end of our finances. Our cupboards were bare. The bills were piling up. I had $5 in my wallet. That was it. The savings account was drained. We knew God had called us to seminary. He had promised to look after our needs. But He was not forthcoming with the finances we so desperately needed. Each day looked a little more bleak than the one preceding it.

I hopped in the van and headed for the grocery store with my $5 bill, complaining all the way. Then I heard Him speak, "Can you thank Me that you have enough for today?"

"Are you kidding me?! What is $5 going to get me? Our cupboards are bare," I retorted. Again He asked the same question. Humbled, I acquiesced. "Yes, Lord, I can thank You."

So I walked through the grocery store. What did I *have* to have for breakfast the next morning? Milk. Eggs. Bread. That would do it. I brought my paltry selection to the till. The cashier totalled my groceries, which added up to just under $5. I had enough. I rejoiced!

The next day I received a surprise in the mail. The government had changed its policy on family allowance and, as a result, was sending the money earlier than normal. Not only was it early, it was much more than they had ever sent before. In the envelope was a cheque for approximately $1,700! It had arrived just on time. Not late. Not early. What had appeared to me as the Lord not listening was just Him waiting, waiting for me to come to a place of humility and trust. I needed to be okay with having enough for the moment. I needed to be grateful for what He was giving me. I needed to be able to say, "Lord, I trust You," even when He was not answering in my time, or in the way I had expected.

Abraham and Sarah did eventually have a baby. And today their descendants are "as numerous as the stars." Elijah did get an answer. The Lord sent fire to burn up his offering and then sent rain to refresh the land. Joseph became second in command to the Pharaoh of Egypt. He ruled over his brothers, and even over his parents. He saved their lives as well as the lives of all the families in Egypt. But in the land between the prayer (or promise) and the answer it did not seem as though God was listening. However, these people never gave up. They continued to trust God. At just the right time, God brought the answer.

When God is silent, maybe He has purposed a better plan. Maybe God has entrusted His silence to us for a greater reason. Maybe it is for the purpose of developing trust in Him. One thing I am learning is that when God is silent, I need to keep doing the last thing He told me to do. At just the right time He will reveal the next step.

Can you trust God, even when everything is dark and bleak? When He is silent? When it seems the wait is just too long? Can you say, along with David the psalmist:

"My heart is confident in you, O God; no wonder I can sing your praises with all my heart!" (Ps 108:1, NLT).

When God is silent let us not lose hope, but have courage to keep on doing the last thing He asked us to do.

SHAKEN TO THE CORE

Charleen Raschke

Disillusion: "to destroy the ideals, illusions or false ideas of" (Dictionary.com, Nov 2018).

There was a time, during a period of healing, when I needed to untangle what was truth from the lies I was believing. I can't even tell you the moment the lies were conceived; they were more like subtleties creeping into my belief system.

Going way back, my relationship with Jesus was vibrant. There was an expectancy that I carried with me. I knew He was good, that He would speak to me, and that He was active all around me. I had never felt more alive! This was an exciting time in my life. I could hardly wait to spend time with Him, every day!

A few years passed by, and these intimate experiences were all woven into my foundation. Then, after one trauma followed by another, involving the lives of two of our children, we were shaken to our cores. My once-vibrant prayer life dwindled to a weak "Help!" We were in the scariest season of our lives.

As our family stumbled along, we sought out counselling and prayer counselling, and I contacted prayer warriors across three provinces. The traumas left a scent of death.

"A thief has only one thing in mind—he wants to steal, slaughter [kill], and destroy…" (John 10:10, TPT).

That is how it felt. The thief stole from us. He tried to kill and destroy us and we felt every bit of that.

As I walked through my healing, I began to see how I needed to disentangle truth from false beliefs. I had picked up a belief somewhere along the way that, because I was close to Jesus, nothing could touch my family. I have no idea where it came from, that's how subtle it was.

Disillusionment is often thought of in a negative light, but in this situation disillusion was what was needed. I needed to dismantle this 'false idea'.

The trauma caused a 'shaking off' of the things that were false. This necessary shaking took me right down to my core beliefs, as I quickly realized that anything else simply didn't matter. The core, Jesus, became the only foundation I needed. The truth is that we are promised trials and suffering, and my family wasn't exempt from that.

As painful as our trauma was, the stripping away of what was false caused me to cling to Jesus more than ever before. This was the silver lining—a deepening of my relationship with Him, and the beauty that encompassed that relationship.

The rest of John 10:10 is often not quoted, and it is the best part!

"...but my desire is to give you everything in abundance, more than you expect—life in its fullness until you overflow!" (TPT)

After experiencing the enemy—the thief—nearly destroying us, I eventually began to see that God's desire was for me to live in His fullness...overflowing.

None of us want to be put to tests or go through horrific events. Yet, if we are willing to keep going, to keep seeking His face in the midst of it all, we can get through it. God wants us all to experience His restoration, His redemptive power at work in our lives—indeed, *life in its overflowing fullness.*

ACCUSED, BUT NOT CONDEMNED

Lynda Blazina

There have been a couple of situations that I have walked through in my life in which I have been accused of things that were not my intention. Accused of having less-than-pure motives. Accused of character flaws that were the perceived motivation for actions I had taken.

On top of much disillusionment surrounding my relationships with the accusers, these situations stung spiritually! The accusations threw me into a place of second-guessing decisions and even my place in ministry. The areas in which I was ministering had been places where I believed God had put me, according to the gifts that He had given me. All of a sudden, they seemed like places of hurt and pain. After one situation in particular I proclaimed to my husband with every fibre of my being, "I will *never* be involved in any sort of women's ministry again … *ever.*"

For many years, I followed that mandate. I would get involved in areas of ministry where I felt competent, and where there wasn't as great a need to be vulnerable with others. This allowed me still to be active in ministry but stay out of the line of fire as far as leadership and making decisions.

There was one problem though. I also wasn't as fulfilled in ministry as I once had been. I knew that I wasn't living in my giftedness. I knew that God had more for me in ministry, but the thought of stepping back into leadership was just too much for my wounded heart. I couldn't wrap my mind around being hurt again.

Through those painful situations, I had bought into a lie. Somewhere along the line, I began to believe that if people accused me of something, I must be doing something wrong.

Years later, my daughter was contemplating leaving an unhealthy relationship. She went to her pastor's wife and started to process things with her. She wisely listened to my daughter pour out her heart, and let her reveal some of the hurtful words and situations that were pushing her to break off the relationship.

Her response was one of godly counsel. She said, "Let me ask you a question. Who is it that is our accuser? Who is it that berates us and knocks us down? Who belittles us and wants to keep us 'small'? It is Satan! I'm not saying that the person is Satan, but I *am* saying that when someone who is supposed to love us is attacking us in a way that Satan would, it is not acceptable!"

After the conversation, they prayed for healing and restoration of Ryshon's spirit, and that she would know the worth and value God had placed on her.

Whoa!

All of a sudden, the words of accusations that had come my direction years before resurfaced. God used that moment and those wise words to my daughter to heal something I had been trying to bury for years—guilt over accusations.

God reminded me of the ways in which He had gifted me, and gently encouraged me to step into my gifts of leadership, discipleship, and teaching once again. He replaced the accuser's voice with one of life-giving healing and power.

Romans 8:1–2 says:

"Therefore, there is now no condemnation for those who are in Christ Jesus, because through Christ Jesus the law of the Spirit who gives life has set you free from the law of sin and death."

This does not mean that we are never in the wrong. Just ask my husband! I still take many missteps and have cranky, sinful days. We, on this side of heaven, will always mess up and get things wrong. However, God's heart is to love and encourage us into the people He created us to be. He wants us to use the gifts and talents that He has given us. He wants to empower us through His Spirit to minister to others in wholeness.

I realized that day that I had been accused by more than people. Satan had taken the opportunity to accuse me, and I had listened. When Jesus revealed the truth, that I was not condemned by *Him* over any of these things, the accusations lost their power over me. Jesus' voice outweighed those of my accusers, and I was suddenly free.

PICTURE PERFECT

Lisa Clarke

A s I got up one morning and headed downstairs, I glanced over at a picture of my two daughters hugging and smiling at the camera. I had a flashback of the day the picture was taken. At a glance this picture looks so perfect. It captures the girls beautifully—but if I am honest it was anything but.

Just hours before that shot was taken, the girls had had words and I didn't know if we could even get them in the same vicinity of each other to get a picture. Since our middle daughter's death, I had been trying to assemble some 'normal' moments. The more I tried to regain something we had as a family, the more things fell apart.

1 Corinthians 10:13 says:

"No temptation has overtaken you except what is common to mankind. And God is faithful; he will not let you be tempted beyond what you can bear. But when you are tempted, he will also provide a way out so that you can endure it."

I had a friend tell me that "God never gives us more than we can handle." I suspect this misconception was birthed out of this passage: God won't allow us to be tempted beyond what we can bear. However, our life circumstances are often *way beyond* what we can handle on our own. Seeing the picture of my girls was a reminder that our family had seen brokenness upon brokenness that we could not handle.

God in His graciousness comes alongside us, and helps us to endure and even praise Him in the storm. That is significantly different than not facing more than we can handle! One perspective is looking for God to completely deliver us from whatever life dishes out. The other remembers, "I will be with you in it. I will not leave you or forsake you."

Deuteronomy 31:6 says:

"Be strong and courageous. Do not be afraid or terrified because of them, for the Lord your God goes with you; he will never leave you nor forsake you."

Hebrews 13:5 says it again:

"Never will I leave you; never will I forsake you."

This is vastly different than thinking that God won't allow really difficult things to happen in our lives. I feel as if we have been duped, thinking that God owes us smooth passage. This life sharpens us to fight falling asleep to the lulls of the world—to be awake and alert. We can easily be put to sleep by the smooth, rhythmic rock of oblivion to this world and its hurt and pain.

As I walk through circumstances that only God is able to control or handle, my cry is "Oh, God, please! Don't let me go to the place of no sun and complete desert, roaming in the dark and trying to find my way back to the Son! Oh, Lord, have mercy."

Then, as the darkness around me dissipates, I feel warmth again. I thank God for His mercies that are new each morning, as Lamentations 3:22–23 says. Then I breathe and am grateful and ask for these subtle reminders that God loves me and my family amidst our brokenness, and that He cares about every aspect of our lives. *With* God, all things are possible—even walking through circumstances I can't handle.

FAITH BUCKET

Deborah Carpenter

When I was a little girl, I would go to my grandparents' farm in Saskatchewan for two weeks every summer. Those weeks were spent outside playing with cousins and farm animals of all sorts and generally getting filthy dirty. The days were long and hot and, by mid-afternoon, my grandmother's kitchen would be filled with sweaty kids desperate for a drink of water. On the kitchen counter, just inside the swinging porch door, was a large plastic bucket filled with the clearest, coolest water and we would dunk in our Tupperware cups and draw up a full glass.

We would take turns, filling and drinking, filling and drinking until we were gasping with satisfaction. Years later, I can still taste it. Cold and sweet, completely refreshing. No drink of water, no matter how fancy, has ever compared to the water from my grandparents' water bucket. And as I recall, that bucket never seemed to be empty. I don't know who kept refilling it. All I know is that when we needed a cold drink, the bucket was there, filled and ready for us to have our fill.

What made that water so sweet? Was it the hotness of the day? The hours of running and jumping and playing that caused our mouths to parch, requiring refreshment? Was it that we hadn't taken time to drink since our morning Tang? Perhaps all of that. Or maybe the water was just, well, sweet.

It has been quite a few years since then, but I remember a time much later in my life when I went looking for a big glass of faith in the bucket of my soul. After my husband's serious accident, our family had to move but we didn't have anywhere to go. We had looked for months for a place to rent, but there was nothing available for such a large family or at a price we could afford. Life had turned into a hot and sticky mess, day after day of stress and turmoil, and my soul was parched. And that bucket was empty. Empty. Not a drop.

"God, it's empty!" I cried. "I knew this would happen! I knew the day would come when I couldn't do this anymore. I knew I was running low, but now there is nothing left!" I felt dark panic begin to rise inside of me.

My phone rang. Could it be a landlord calling to say we had been approved for a house? No. Instead it was a lady from my church calling to see if I would share my story with the ladies' group that was meeting for an Easter tea. Ironic.

Sweetie, are you sure you want me to speak? You see, my dear, you are going to get a Good Friday message, and not an Easter Morning message. It won't be the feel-good message you might expect.

For some reason, she stood firm.

Yes, please come. We'd love to hear from you.

And so, I agreed.

I hung up the phone and sat down. Oh, Lord. What am I going to do? I have no business speaking to these women. And besides, in case you haven't noticed, my faith bucket is empty.

"Look again," He said.

"What?"

"Look. Again."

So I did. And there, at the very bottom of that bucket, I found a little more faith. Strange. I was sure it was empty a few hours ago. So, I looked again and there was a little bit more. I tentatively dipped in my cup and drew it up. Miraculously, my cup was full. And the water was sweet, so very sweet.

Our Father God asks us in Psalm 34:8 to "taste and see that the LORD is good." To truly taste His goodness, I must first go to the source of that goodness. This might be done through a desperate prayer, as I prayed. It might be in a stolen moment of quiet contemplation as I survey the day ahead and wonder how I am going to make it through. But I come to a God who is good. A God who longs to revive the weary and lift the head of the weak.

Every day, one of my grandparents went to the well and drew up water to fill the counter bucket. They knew there would be thirsty children clamouring for a drink. They knew the days were long and hot, and they knew we would need refreshing. I knew that if that bucket was ever empty, it wouldn't be empty for long.

And like my grandparents, God knows I need refreshing too. He fills that bucket day by day with His goodness. He simply asks that I come and drink.

41

Lynda Blazina

As I sat at the kitchen table in the quiet house, with Mom sleeping in her room, hot tears began to flow down my face. They were tears that came from brokenness and feeling completely overwhelmed. I had been driving several hours to be Mom's primary caretaker during her battle with cancer. Things were progressing as the doctors said they would, and I knew that Mom wouldn't be with us long.

Though I had become caretaker, life at home hadn't been put on hold. In spite of my not being present, we were in the midst of dealing with several other life circumstances that weighed heavy on my heart. So many things were taking place at once that it was difficult to catch my breath. The Bible speaks of sorrow upon sorrow. That described my soul all too well.

This season of suffering was getting old! I was tired and worn, and I longed to have some happiness return to my life. My shoulders were carrying all that I could handle and I felt myself slipping into the abyss of depression.

As I sat at the kitchen table pouring my heart out to the Lord, all of a sudden I heard what was being said on the TV that my mom had turned on earlier.

"Your 41 is coming."

I thought of all the stories in the Bible that this short statement was referencing. Noah endured 40 days of rain. The Israelites spent 40 years in the wilderness. Jesus was tempted for 40 days.

I stopped!

I grabbed my new journalling Bible and wrote a large '41' on one of the pages, and then cried some more. New tears of thankfulness, knowing that the Lord had seen and heard my sorrow and had given me a very direct message.

My 41 was coming.

Over the next couple of years there were many moments of pain and continued suffering, but always, at just the right time as I flipped through my Bible or went to read a particular passage, the pages would fall open to that '41.' I would whisper a quick prayer of thankfulness that the Lord had once again heard my sorrowful cries and reminded me of the promise He had given me back when my mom was dying.

A promise of redemption and healing. A promise of dry land, the promised land. A promise of change and transformation. Because of Jesus, I could have hope during the dark days of my current 40, knowing that, inevitably, God would turn the page to 41.

I believe I am entering a season of my 41. Things are more joyful; days are brighter. Not always easy, not always happy, but I am aware of God's faithfulness and His workings in my life more and more. If you are currently in a season of pain and hardship, know that God never allows pain without purpose. Even if you are in the darkest of circumstances that you did not cause, know that God can use those circumstances to glorify Himself. Because of God's kindness and His love for you, know that your 41 will come.

"Because of the LORD's great love we are not consumed, for his compassions never fail. They are new every morning; great is your faithfulness" (Lam 3:22–23).

REST AND REFLECTION

Your Name

If you were 100% honest with God, what is an area of your life that you would ask Him to help you with?

Write out a prayer, asking Jesus to come into these areas of your life, and show you ways that you can trust Him and His work in these areas.

WINTER STORM

Betty Siemens Martens

Snowflakes, soft, white, fluffy snowflakes
Falling gently, no sound they make.
A beautiful, feathery sight.
'Tis the picture of pure delight.
Soon comes along a playful breeze
Those fluffy snowflakes to chase and tease.
They dance, they twirl, they spin around
Then come to rest upon the ground.
Not for long; the wind increases
All its fury it releases.
Whipping the snow across the field
And all around, its power to wield.
Then in the night the wind retires,
While in the house they stoke the fires.
The stars come out. Oh, how they shimmer!
'Til morning light makes them dimmer.
The sun comes out in full glory,
The trees they glisten white and hoary.
Drifts of snow like diamonds galore!
Awesome sight! Calm reigns once more.
So is the storm within the soul
Who will not let God take control.
But perfect peace comes in to stay
When Christ the Saviour leads the way.

ANGEL IN DISGUISE

Brenda Goudy

"Lord, all my desire is before You; and my sighing is not hidden from you" (Ps 38:9, NAS).

"The Lord doesn't see things the way you see them. People judge by outward appearance, but the Lord looks at the heart" (1 Sam 16:7b, NLT).

He was no angel. Or was he? Certainly, no teacher had ever accused him of it. I will always wonder if perhaps he was an angel in disguise. At the very least he was a gift given from God, and he changed my life. Those are big words and big emotions to attach to a 13-year-old junior high boy, and I certainly didn't expect him to affect my life in the way he did. But God doesn't always work in the ways we expect Him to.

I had been working part-time as an Educational Assistant at a private Christian school for two years when the opportunity for full-time hours came up. I had been in the early elementary department my first years there, and was fully convinced that it was the only place for me. I needed full-time hours so this was an answer to prayer…with one catch. I would be half-time in grade 3 and half-time in junior high, mostly with grade 7. I was terrified, and my first thought was "Absolutely not!" I was convinced that I would hate working with teens, and they would certainly hate me. At the same time, I desperately needed the hours so I determined to "Do my work as unto the Lord" and simply hate my job for half the day, every day.

It didn't take long to see where I would be most needed in that classroom. The skinny, dark-haired boy, with the face of an angel and a devilish glint in his eye, would be my primary responsibility. As sweet as he looked, his behaviour revealed the opposite, although every disruption was offered with a cheeky grin and a twinkle in his eye. Love him or hate him, this boy set the tone for the whole class, and I knew I would have to win him over if I was to have any place with the students in that class.

It took some time, a few pranks, and a lot of patience to win him over, and he pushed the limits in making me prove that I truly liked him unconditionally and would not stop or give up on him. Authority was not a welcome guest in his life; most of his school experience was that of being punished and he often felt disliked. After a few weeks of testing the waters, along with a delicious prank that I pulled on him in front of all his peers, we became unlikely best friends.

This occurred during the darkest time of my separation, divorce proceedings, and struggle to capture and keep the hearts of my own boys. During that time, I tried my best to believe that my boys would never choose to be apart from me and that their hearts would not be turned against me, but deep inside I wondered and worried that it could happen.

The pain of uncertainty in my relationship with my boys was excruciating, and many days I did not think I could get out of bed and carry out my day. My rescue came from the most unlikely of places: that 13-year-old boy and his classmates.

Once I had established my place in their lives, they welcomed me with open arms. My sadness and fear of possibly losing my close relationship with my own boys created what I like to call a 'teenage-boy-shaped hole in my heart.' That hole was filled by these boys and girls in the junior high classroom. Many days my only motivation to put myself together and get through the day was found in the knowledge that thirty faces would light up when I walked into the classroom. A seat would always be saved for me by my new buddy and, come semester changes and grade changes, I would be given their class schedule so I could find them on my breaks. Their love and acceptance and simply wanting to spend time with me was the healing love that I needed.

Time has passed, and my own boys and I are very close. Our relationship was not destroyed. In addition, I still have a close relationship with many of the students from that grade 7 class, now in university. I know, without reservation, that God brought them all into my life at just the right time, and while I helped them in the classroom, they helped me just as much. My 'angel' friend and I have developed a deep and loyal friendship that remains to this day.

As unlikely as that may be, God doesn't always work in ways that make sense to us. While many people saw him as a trouble-making kid, God saw him as a young man with a heart that would reach out to a lady he didn't know needed him. God knew the desires of my own heart to be loved and needed by an extra 'son' during the times I was disconnected from my own. An angel? His professors and parents may disagree, but I will always wonder.

CAUGHT IN THE SURF

Connie Lucille Peachey

We were in Africa visiting our international workers. There were eight of us on the team. A friend wanted to treat us to a day on the beach, so we boarded what I would call a questionable sea vessel. But everyone was using them, so we figured it was likely safe. We hugged the shore as we made our way around the point to a lovely secluded little resort of quaint cottages and an open-air restaurant. The sand was exquisite. The sun was hot. Exactly my idea of a perfect day in a perfect place.

As we ate our lunch, the tide started coming in. Those waves beckoned to me—I love body surfing the waves. After lunch we all went down to the beach and got our umbrellas set up and our towels all laid out. Then we headed into the water. It was glorious! I played in the waves until my energy began to wane. As I headed back toward land for a rest, I realized that the waves had gotten much bigger than they were when we had first started to play in them.

I was almost to shore when a wave sneaked up behind me and knocked me down. As I tried to scramble to my feet, the same wave knocked me down again on its way back out to sea, this time pulling my top lower than what was acceptable on that beach among other ministry colleagues. I scrambled to pull my top up while trying to gain my footing. Another wave came crashing over me, taking my feet right out from under me again. I was losing strength. As I held my top with one hand, I tried to push myself up with the other. That stupid wave came back down the beach and swept me right back off my feet. This happened over and over again. I was stuck in some nightmarish vortex from which I just could not pull myself.

Then James came along. In his gentle manner he asked if I needed a bit of help.

Was my swim suit up far enough? Had he seen anything he should not see? Oh dear. Yes, I did in fact need some help. He reached out his hand and helped me up. It was simple with his strength added to mine. Well, mine was gone, so it was mostly his. But, with his encouragement and his hand, I was able to stand up and walk to my towel. I flopped, totally spent, onto the sand, allowing the sun to warm me and waiting for my pulse to calm down and my breathing to regulate. Were it not for James, I would still be tumbling in the surf in some far-off region of Africa.

This last week felt just like that experience. The events of the week were not necessarily all bad. Well, our friends' house fire was awful. But there were many other glorious things going on—opportunities to minister to others, seeing God at work in the lives of those around me. But events just kept slamming me down, demanding my time and energy. My nights were shortened and days lengthened. Just when I thought I was going to get a break, another event pushed its way into my day. This began on Saturday, and it took me until Wednesday to finally realize that I had forgotten to ask Jesus for help in navigating these interruptions. I was just like a two-year-old saying "I can do it myself!"

On my way home from one of these events I pulled the car over. Jesus had been gently calling to me, asking, "Do you need any help? Here, take My hand." But I had been too busy trying to hold myself together lest someone think me inept. Finally, I called out, "Jesus, please be 'James' for me. Be my breakwater. Take my hand. Help me." And, just like that, His peace came flooding in. The week looming before me was just as busy, with nary a break in activity. But everything changed. Now I was not doing it alone. Now I was not overwhelmed by the waves knocking me down. Jesus was taking the brunt of the waves. He took me by the hand and together we began walking out of the fray into a place of shalom.

"Peace I leave with you; my peace I give you. I do not give to you as the world gives. Do not let your hearts be troubled and do not be afraid" (John 14:27).

"I have told you these things, so that in me you may have peace. In this world you will have trouble. But take heart! I have overcome the world" (John 16:33).

"But you, O LORD, are a shield around me; you are my glory, the one who holds my head high" (Ps 3:3, NLT).

Are you caught in the surf? Is life throwing you down and tumbling you head over heels? Can you see Jesus' hand reaching for yours and hear His gentle offer of assistance? Do not be afraid. He is waiting for you to admit you need His help. He may not necessarily remove the obstacles or struggles but He will walk *with* you, filling you with His strength and courage and peace.

WHEN ALL I CAN SAY

Kerry Robideau

"Therefore I will boast all the more gladly of my weaknesses, so that the power of Christ may rest upon me" (2 Cor 12:9b, ESV).

"Help!" That was my only prayer. I couldn't pray another word because there were no more words. I was too broken and too empty.

It was during a summer holiday, on the first day as we were setting up camp, that I heard the Holy Spirit whisper to me Psalm 23:1: "The Lord is my shepherd, I lack nothing."

"What did that mean, Lord?"

It was a verse I had memorized as a child; it might have been one of the first verses I had memorized. Now it was staring me in the face, leaving me to wonder what I would need shepherding for. What would be lacking?

Just before we had headed out for holidays, a church member decided that my husband was no longer fit to lead the church as pastor. We knew there were a few people talking behind our backs. We also knew there were more people who were for us, but who were too afraid to stand up for what was right. When we returned from our holiday, the leaders against us saw fit to make our life miserable, and they did their best to oust my husband from the pulpit and from his position as pastor.

The year-long battle that followed broke us. I didn't feel like I lacked nothing; I felt I was lacking everything!

"What did You mean, Lord?" We resigned, feeling empty.

Moving back to my hometown with our children didn't change the emptiness we felt. If anything, it changed the playing field of the battle from the external to the internal. Guilt, shame, fear, hopelessness, worthlessness, loneliness, and isolation all crept their way into our hearts and minds. The battle had quieted on the outside but was roaring on the inside.

"Jesus, what did You mean that we would lack nothing?"

As a wife, mother, daughter, and friend I didn't have much to offer anyone. Anything I did have to offer went to my growing boys and my dying mother who had been diagnosed with terminal cancer.

"God's grace is sufficient; I lack nothing!"

God's grace doesn't always look like what we want it to look like. Our expectations about our situation and about God were different than His. We expected that He would rescue us, and that truth and righteousness would win out in the end. We expected that the 'bad guys' would be gone and we would stay. It didn't happen that way. Although we didn't get what we wanted or what we thought we deserved, we did learn some very valuable lessons. The experience changed our character, and our faith became more authentic.

What did His grace provide? His grace gave us the right time to leave. Had we tried to move a year earlier as we had wanted to, we wouldn't have been able to get the amount of equity out of our home that we did. His grace provided loyal support for us in the midst of crisis. Through the situation, people came forward who would uphold us in prayer and encouragement. His grace provided healing and godly insights, both in the middle of the storm and after we left, through counselling and prayer ministry. My husband preached some of his best sermons in our last six months there, even though broken. God's grace provided jobs for both of us after we moved.

When you feel weak, God's grace is enough. It is okay to feel that you don't have it all together, to give yourself permission to grieve the losses, and to give yourself time to heal. He will provide, and He is not bound to your limitations and weaknesses, regardless of how you feel. That's what His love for you is all about!

I CAN'T HANDLE THIS

Lynda Blazina

I remember clearly the day my heart broke. I had already endured a lot up to that point. Sorrow upon sorrow had flooded my life and after hearing one more piece of news, even though it wasn't an incredibly huge thing, life crashed in on me.

I sat outside, away from the eyes and ears of my family, and fell apart. I had become pretty good at carrying stress and grief. I had mastered walking through, in spite of, around, and in the midst of pain. Until that day.

I sobbed. The kind of tears that seem to have no end, from the kind of pain that seems to have no bottom. Just when I would gather myself for a moment, a new depth of sorrow would break to the surface. It was the type of emotional pain that hurts physically. I wanted to throw up. I wanted to just stop breathing because it hurt to take breath or expel it.

I had reached the bottom. In anger, sorrow, grief and frustration I gritted my teeth and said, "God. I. Can't. Handle. This. *Please*…I can't handle this…I cannot handle this."

Over and over I repeated the words as my tears kept falling.

Brokenness. That is what I felt. Completely undone. At the end of all that I had within me. Done with any pretences of holding life together or having any sort of sanity reserves. I was done.

Exhausted and beyond words, I sat in numbness for the next hour or so. As someone who constantly has something running through my mind, it was too quiet to enjoy. At the same time, I didn't have the energy to care that the sudden quiet was almost disturbing either.

After sitting in the ache of heartbreak for a while longer, I whispered one more time with much less emotion, "I can't handle this anymore."

The quiet response crashed into my silence: "Who asked you to?"

Pardon??

"*Who* asked you to handle it? I didn't."

Again...*Pardon?*

"Of course you can't handle it. I never created you to handle it. The weight you are trying to bear is too much for any person to handle. That is what I AM here for. I can and will handle it, but you have got to let go of 'it' if you want Me to carry the burden of your world for you."

Huh.

That was literally my response.

After taking a second to process and comprehend what I believe was the Lord's intervening voice, my response was a little more wordy, if not more spiritual. It went something like this:

"'Okay, God, You have to handle it then. If I give it to You, You have to take it. Please take it. Please handle every little nuance and itty bitty piece of pain and sorrow that I'm carrying. Please take it all and do with it what I know in my head *only* You can do with it."

The pain lifted. The tap of tears that had been incessant stopped.

Just processing the fact that I didn't have to carry the burdens of my little world on *my* shoulders—that God wanted to do that *for* me—was enough. Enough to surrender my want to control things and navigate in my own strength. Enough to hand it over, even though I knew this would be a process that I would have to repeat daily.

"Cast your cares on the Lord and he will sustain you; he will never let the righteous be shaken" (Ps 55:22).

"Humble yourselves, therefore, under God's mighty hand, that he may lift you up in due time. Cast all your anxiety on him because he cares for you" (1 Pet 5:6–7).

"Come to me, all you who are weary and burdened, and I will give you rest" (Matt 11:28).

When I surrender my desire to be lord of my world, when I am able to be broken and a bit of a disaster in His loving and gentle presence, I am always able to go on. I can go on, knowing that my God, the God of all strength, is handling it for me.

PAIN HEAPED UPON PAIN

Charleen Raschke

For several years I was stuck in a cycle of mild pain, which then turned into moderate pain, and finally excruciating, debilitating pain. I was a mess in far too many ways, in the throes of emotional anguish as well as physical pain.

It hadn't always been this way. There had been a long season previously of vibrancy and excitement as we walked with God and our church community.

But here we were. Dealing with more wreckage after going through the worst storms we had ever experienced.

"Dear friends, do not be surprised at the painful trial you are suffering, as though something strange were happening to you" (1 Pet 4:12).

We had sold our little bungalow and bought a storey-and-a-half house in a more desirable neighbourhood, situated beside amazing paved walking and biking trails. This place—this time—looked so hopeful. We longed for easier days and seasons.

The hard work of moving, unpacking, and repainting our new place was all a part of making it feel like home to us. The energy to do the work came with trickles of hope for something better. We started to heal emotionally. Hope began returning to us.

In the year that followed, I was happy to walk my dog alongside my husband as he pushed our son in his wheelchair. But by the end of that summer I could no longer ignore the mild pain, as it had turned into excruciating limps. Our walks came to a very sad end. My heart was crushed once again. As if it wasn't hard enough for my husband and me to have to consider every place we went with a wheelchair in tow, now this too? My sad began to mix with mad. This felt like another injustice.

I changed doctors. The first doctor I had seen did nothing about my pain and increasing loss of motion. I needed another opinion. What was happening to me?

I was only in my early forties, so when we finally got my diagnosis it was quite a blow. I would not need one major surgery, but two! I had a genetic condition, and apparently nothing could have prevented this outcome. My bones were misshaped, which had caused them to wear down my cartilage much sooner than they should have. I needed one complete hip replacement and one hip reconstruction.

Nights were the worst. I needed anti-inflammatories, pain killers and sleeping pills to get through a night … every night. The pain would throb down both of my legs almost all night long.

I lost range of motion and a lot of strength. I couldn't walk far at all. I limped quite badly. Pain messed with my head. It was difficult for me to read or concentrate on much of anything. My life looked like a crash site!

This season lasted around five years, from the time of my increased pain until my last surgery and final recuperation.

Hope and faith were replenished by receiving prayer and encouragement from others and from the Lord. Eventually, our gaping wounds did heal. It was never fast, but with each step forward, through the pain, we were healed and restored.

Jesus is faithful! He revealed this part of His character to us through these trials. He promises to never leave us, and we can honestly say that He never did. When we look back at that time, we see His grace, we see His love, we see His fingerprints. We may not have always felt His presence, but that doesn't change the truth that He was with us (Deut 31:6).

"The Lord is close to the brokenhearted and saves those who are crushed in spirit" (Ps 34:18).

REST AND REFLECTION

Your Name

So often we read something that resonates with us and unless we write it down and/or share it with someone, it often slips to the back of our minds never to be implemented.

What has stirred your heart this week?

What is one thing you need to change to experience greater intimacy with Jesus?

Who will you tell?

LIVING THE DREAM

Lynda Blazina

There were many days, as I walked through my seasons of winter, when the thought "How can this be my life?" flitted through (and sometimes parked in) my mind. Nothing in my life was going the way I wanted it to. Nothing felt happy or joyful. There were many days when I felt like I was running this marathon of life through waist-deep snow.

One day in the midst of the 'snow,' I saw a familiar verse in a completely different way. This is often how the Lord speaks to me—through new perspectives on things I have always seen a certain way.

The verse that He brought to mind was "Now to Him who is able to do above and beyond all that we ask or imagine, according to the power that works in us" (Eph 3:20, CSB).

The difference was subtle.

I had always thought of this verse as saying that no matter how big my dreams are, He can use them and expand them and go even further with them than I could. If I could imagine success in a certain area that I believed was a godly dream, He could take that and give me even more success in that area *and* in other areas that I hadn't even thought to ask for. He would give success…but they would still be my dreams.

Then God placed this thought on my heart: What if My dreams for you are *better* than the plans you have imagined? And what if My plans for you are *better* than the dreams you have pictured?

Our plans and dreams are based on the things that we are capable of picturing. This means that our dreams are limited to ideas that are formulated from our experiences. When I picture a 'happy' life, I picture all the things that I can imagine making me happy from the things I've observed in life—the storybook endings and the movie-worthy love; the Instagram picture-perfect children and Pinterest-worthy home.

But what if the plans and dreams that Jesus holds in His hands for me look different? What if they look like prayer ministry for a mom whose heart has been broken? Or speaking freedom into the lives of women who are living in bondage? Or walking with young women who haven't discovered their identities and are living in despair? Or encouraging healing in marriages that are ready to implode? What if God was allowing me to go through all this pain because He has great plans for using every second of it?

What if Jesus' dreams for me aren't about the here and now of *happy*, but the deep and eternal things of *joy*? What if all that I can ask or imagine is far less than Jesus?

I started asking the Holy Spirit to reveal His dreams for me—His dreams that went far wider and deeper than my human heart knew to dream. Eternal dreams.

I began to realize that many of my broken 'dreams' were just faltering fantasies. God had given this life to me and had purpose and design for the things that I was walking through. My worthless broken dreams were building a platform of eternal value.

This *was* more than I could think of or imagine. It went far beyond the narrow scope of the dreams I had for my life. This new perspective of God's truth allowed me to step into trusting His dreams for me. When I realized that all my brokenness and mess had purpose, I could find joy in living the dream.

TRUST

Stefanie Carlson

Patience can be the most frustrating thing to learn. In my experience, waiting leaves me feeling like I have a ball of anxiety sitting in my throat. I just want to *do* something—anything to make the waiting go quicker, or to have an answer right away.

I feel this in so many different aspects of my business, personal, financial, and even emotional life right now. My husband Drew made a big switch last August. It had been months in coming. With stress and debt circling overhead, threatening to swallow us whole at any given moment, Drew made the decision to close his company of 13-plus years and liquidate his business. He had absorbed many losses over the past three years, and had even had to take legal action against clients who attempted to walk away from invoices. He fought long and hard for his company to survive and, after years of successes and failures, he finally made the decision to walk away. He had to leave everything and start something new, unknown and at the bottom.

We both knew he should be in sales. He is amazing with people and easy to talk to. We knew he could use his past experience working in the trades to his advantage in his new career: real estate.

In true Drew fashion, he set high goals to achieve within a short timeline. He wanted to prove to himself and his team that he would be the best and the quickest. He finished school in only two and a half months. But it became clear that this chapter of life wasn't meant to be about getting stuff done. It was about the painful ache of waiting.

We learned that, no matter how much of a go-getter you are or how confident you are that you are making the right decisions, sometimes timing doesn't match up to expectations and goals. Sometimes you are forced to be patient.

"Patience is also a form of action." — August Rodin

Between finishing up his schooling and the time of this writing, Drew still hasn't been paid. It's been several months since his last pay cheque, and we've had to come up with money to front the cost of re-altor fees, to survive Christmas, a few birthdays, and to pay back some loans. We have had so much support and encouragement from our family and friends. As an added bonus, Drew is good at his job! However, we are still in the middle of the waiting game—my least favourite game of all time.

We are forced to live completely in faith. We know that the finances are coming—he has done the work and is sitting on four home sales—but we don't know when the first cheque will come. It could be this afternoon, or tomorrow. It could be another few weeks. A part of me wants to scream. Another part of me wants to get a loan. But I am choosing to believe that just staying in this place of uncertainty, surrendered in patience, is a form of action. It is action in that we are choosing not to be swayed. We are choosing to hold onto our positivity.

How blessed we are that we arrived at the point of certainty that Drew needed to make a career change. In that new career, we are already thanking God for the sales. He is blessing us and we will continue to proclaim how blessed we are. God is never late, and rarely early.

"For the revelation awaits an appointed time; it speaks of the end and will not prove false. Though it linger, wait for it; it will certainly come and will not delay" (Hab 2:3).

The word 'patience' refers to the willingness to stay where we are and live the current situation to the full, in the belief that something hidden will manifest itself. In our case, we know that this is a short season. Even if I don't know how we will pay our mortgage, our savings are gone, and our rule to "Pay off the credit cards each month" is a laugh.

We are coming to the point where the limits are scary close, but I know that this will pass. I just need to let go of my need to know *when*.

I encourage you in your seasons to be willing to see the lesson in the waiting. Instead of reflecting only after surviving a hard season, attempt to find purpose while in it. Every time I practise this, peace encompasses me even if the situation hasn't changed.

"For everything there is a season, and a time for every matter under heaven:

a time to be born, and a time to die;
a time to plant, and a time to pluck up what is planted;
a time to kill, and a time to heal;
a time to break down, and a time to build up;
a time to weep, and a time to laugh;
a time to mourn, and a time to dance;
a time to cast away stones, and a time to gather stones together;
a time to embrace, and a time to refrain from embracing;
a time to seek, and a time to lose;
a time to keep, and a time to cast away;
a time to tear, and a time to sew;
a time to keep silence, and a time to speak;
a time to love, and a time to hate;
a time for war, and a time for peace" (Eccles 3:1–8, ESV).

God's timing is always perfect. Trust His perfect timing.

FREE IN THE TRUTH

Amy Cordell

"If we confess our sins, He is faithful and just to forgive us our sins and to cleanse us from all unrighteousness" (1 John 1:9). "Repent then, and turn to God, so that your sins may be wiped out, that times of refreshing may come from the Lord" (Acts 3:19).

"'Come now, let us settle the matter,' says the Lord, 'Though your sins are like scarlet, they shall be white as snow; though they are crimson, they shall be like wool'" (Isa 1:18).

As we sat in the room with the marriage counsellor, I froze as my then-husband announced that, because I was his wife, I deserved whatever treatment he gave me and was required to stay married to him at any cost.

At that moment I knew that whatever the counsellor said next would shape my decision for the future. I was at the end of my rope, felt no hope, and was unsure of my ability to know and recognize truth. This counsellor was a respected, godly man and I would accept his opinion as truth.

If the counsellor agreed with him, my then-husband would wield the power of those words over me for the rest of my life. He would tell everyone who would listen that the counsellor supported him. If the counsellor did not agree, then I knew I would feel a freedom that I was so longing for—the freedom to embrace what I already knew in my heart, that I was not deserving of the treatment and situation I was in.

"And don't you think she has regretted that decision every day? Don't you think she has punished herself with that belief every day since?"

I felt a little spark of hope. Maybe there was a way out. Maybe I could someday be free of the prison I found myself in.

At the end of that session, the counsellor asked for a private session with me, to which I agreed. My husband made no secret of the fact that he was sure I was going to be told that I needed to submit and everything would be fine. I would surely be told that I was crazy and that he was a longsuffering saint for putting up with me and my ingratitude. I, however, knew differently. The little spark of hope had ignited and I was confident that help was going to come.

There have been a few times in my life that I have heard a phrase or had a conversation that changed the way I lived, thought and believed. That private session was one of those moments. The counsellor said to me, "Amy, have you considered that you are punishing yourself for sin that God forgave you for a long time ago?"

With that, the floodgates were opened. God had already forgiven me, so long ago, before I even got married. The sad reality was that I had married my husband out of guilt, believing that I had to face the consequences of my sin, when I had already been forgiven!

After that conversation, I began working on forgiving myself. While I knew the truth that all I had to do was accept that forgiveness and embrace it, I still felt like I didn't *deserve* to be let off the hook so easily. I knew the truth, and yet failed to make the connection to my heart that was needed to live in freedom.

A friend gently confronted me about this one day, saying that, by holding onto that guilt and insisting on punishing myself I was saying that Jesus isn't enough. His sacrifice on the cross didn't quite cover it. I needed to make sure I was punished enough before I could be forgiven. Of course, that sounded ridiculous, and yet it was completely true regarding to how I was living. If God says I am forgiven and clean in His eyes, then it's done.

I finally stepped into the freedom Jesus offered, and left the abusive marriage.

Forgiving my ex-husband was not the difficult part of my healing, especially since I had felt for so long that I was simply facing the consequences of my sin and poor choices. The gratitude I felt for being freed from him and his control was so powerful that it overshadowed any unforgiveness I might have been harbouring. He could treat me however he wanted—God had me. God surrounded me with friends who would walk alongside me no matter what my ex tried to do to discredit me.

Forgiving myself for my sin and all the poor choices I had made out of guilt was harder. However, the Holy Spirit, who is the Comforter, one day whispered to my heart, "It's time." Time to let the feelings of unworthiness fade and step into the peace and love and acceptance that God had offered me all along.

Forgiving myself for choosing him to be the father of my kids has been a struggle. I chose to have children with the poorest choice I could have made—the most angry, destructive, and selfish person I have ever encountered. Our lives have included a struggle and fight for self-worth, independence and freedom. They didn't ask for this or deserve it. I know that if he wasn't their father then *they* wouldn't be here, but the mother mind isn't always rational! And yet, God in His goodness has allowed me to have a deep and authentic relationship with my kids. He has also given each of my kids a deep desire to follow the Lord. We work through life together and join together in dealing with their dad, and my many apologies to them have always been met with complete forgiveness and love.

Forgiveness may not come easily when it comes to forgiving ourselves, but God offers it freely to all who come in repentance and seek Him. Christ's death on the cross was enough, and His grace is enough to heal the most guilty and hurting heart, even if we don't feel like we deserve it. True freedom comes from embracing His love and forgiveness and moving forward in our true identity: a chosen, valued, and beloved child of God.

WINTER

Angelina Sorgen

Sorrowful birds sing summer's exit
As tree leaves wither
Fading from evergreen to hazel
Disintegrating into the earth
You look up and see the somber sky
For the birds have taken the summer south with them
Fragments of the heavens descending upon us
All pieces unique in design
Earth absorbing the first fall of white
Each snowflake melting at first touch
Inhaled: Breath is sharp
Exhaled: Breath is hazy
Your bones stiff from the frigid temperatures
Still, you stand in the whirling winter wonderland
Seeing God's mercies new every morning
Just like the snow that never fails to come

WHEN WILL I SEE YOU AGAIN?

Kerry Robideau

"**N**ow is your time of grief, but I will see you again and you will rejoice, and no one will take away your joy" (John 16:22).

It started with a dream. I dreamed that I had a red-headed baby boy in my arms. The white cloth he was wrapped in only covered his body and not his head. I hadn't seen my baby in full yet so I took off the cloth to give him a good looking over. What I saw was not nice, as his little body was very deformed and his insides were on the outside of his body. I wrapped him back up to keep him warm, then held him close to my body so he would feel my love for him. Then I awoke.

I awoke! No…no…no! I couldn't be pregnant! The only other time I had dreamed about babies was when I was pregnant, upon conception. Could it be true?

A month and a half passed and I found out that I was, or had been, pregnant. The doctor wasn't sure, as I was hemorrhaging and had been for a several weeks already, not realizing that I was not just having my period. While waiting for an internal scan to see what was happening with the baby, the bleeding increased and pain shot up into my left shoulder, indicating internal bleeding. My husband was told by my doctor to take me straight to the hospital in the nearby city; she would phone ahead to the gynecologist who would meet me in the emergency room. She suspected we were dealing with an ectopic pregnancy.

My husband and I had the moral and ethical discussion of what we would do if the baby was still there but threatening my life, when the gynecologist walked in, reassuring us that he would do everything possible to keep everyone safe.

The morning after surgery, the doctor explained to me that the baby was already gone, but that they had found the placenta, the size of my pinky fingernail, inside my left tube which was causing the hemorrhage.

Baby was gone before we even knew he existed. Though there were so many emotions already going on during this time, our hearts hurt over the loss. People around us weren't sure how to respond, many minimizing the loss. "After all, the baby wasn't even past the first trimester; not much baby there." However, to us it was all baby, a person designed in God's own image; our child.

Our grief was real, but because of the reactions of people around us we weren't sure how deeply we were supposed to or allowed to grieve. What was acceptable? Would it be overkill to grieve as deeply as we wanted or needed to?

It took friends who had experienced a similar loss to give us permission to grieve. They came for a visit with no knowledge of what had happened, but ministered deeply to us by allowing us to talk about it and by grieving the loss of our child with us. It was like salve to our souls to have someone understand.

Later that year, the Lord gave me a nudge to ask how our baby boy was doing. He said that he was waiting for us and that his name was Jeremy, which means "whom Jehovah has appointed or exalted." We know from the Bible that Jeremiah the prophet was appointed, but that he was also known as a man of sorrows because of his many troubles. Our Jeremy is a little prophet of sorrows with his troubles and ours.

The verse from John 16 is Jesus' words as He speaks to His disciples about the crucifixion and the sorrow His disciples will encounter. He likens it, in the verse previous, to a woman in labour about to give birth, and the sorrow she encounters in the process until the baby is born.

When He returns there will be joy, just like when a baby is born, the mother's sorrow turns to joy. For some of us, the baby's birth doesn't bring joy but sorrow.

Jesus promises us that our grief is not forever. It's a season in our lives and, at the end, joy will come. The little ones we have never seen on earth we will one day see, for they are waiting for us. God's giving our baby a name tells me that every child not brought to full-term is still highly valued by Him. They were thought of and created by the hand of Jesus Himself (Isa 43:7). They are loved.

I don't claim to understand it all, but for some reason, only fully known to God, going through that experience was important. If, by our encouraging other parents who have gone through similar losses, Jeremy's life has meaning and brings glory to God, he is appointed and exalted as his name attests. We look forward to seeing him again on the other side of heaven, where he waits for us to join him. Then our joy will be made complete!

"There is no foot too small that it cannot leave an imprint on this world" – printed on the memorial picture honouring the Duggars' miscarried child.

A PICTURE OF GRACE

Lisa Clarke

Picture this scene: a young girl of 13, on her knees with her hands raised high asking God for grace. Her words echo in my mind, "O Lord, I need You; please Lord, give me grace!" This memory of my daughter is a reminder to me of many biblical stories. The one to which it points me the most is the story of the publican and the Pharisee in Luke 18:9–14:

To some who were confident of their own righteousness and looked down on everyone else, Jesus told this parable:

"Two men went up to the temple to pray, one a Pharisee and the other a tax collector. The Pharisee stood by himself and prayed: 'God, I thank you that I am not like other people—robbers, evildoers, adulterers—or even like this tax collector. I fast twice a week and give a tenth of all I get.'

"But the tax collector stood at a distance. He would not even look up to heaven, but beat his breast and said, 'God, have mercy on me, a sinner.' I tell you that this man, rather than the other, went home justified before God. For all those who exalt themselves will be humbled, and those who humble themselves will be exalted."

My daughter's heart cries remind me of several things in relationship to this story: Jesus is against those who look down on everyone else, Jesus shows that true prayer brings nothing to the table, and Jesus exalts the humble.

1. Those Jesus Is Against

A picture of grace is someone who doesn't look down on others. This seems so obvious, does it not? Or is it? How subtle are the daily struggles to make ourselves look better to others. To do that, we often put people down—not overtly of course, but in small and subtle ways. How hard should it be to give a pure word of encouragement? For some reason, we think it is our job to make other people change, and we forget the words that Jesus said.

I am thankful for my daughter's life, for the many things she did to make me smile, and for her overwhelming enthusiasm over the things she saw I did for her. She encouraged without feeling superior or looking down on others.

2. True Prayer Has Empty Hands

I see Melissa in Jesus' parable. She was the one in our family who recognized her inability to 'be good.' She was an underachiever who felt lost in the school system, and would often get down on herself because she felt she could never measure up. Ironically, the story of the publican's life and words were also hers: "Lord, have mercy on me, a sinner."

Like the great old hymn says, "Nothing in my hands I bring, simply to the cross I cling." This is another picture of grace given to me by Melissa's prayer.

3. The Humble Are Exalted

When the haunting voices come and make me wonder about Melissa, I am comforted by the words of Jesus. His Kingdom is one where the humble are exalted and the lowly are lifted up; those with nothing to offer are the ones He exalts.

A scene from *The Lord of the Rings* shows a whole company of heroes bending the knee to the lowly hobbits. I remember the delight in Melissa's eyes to see that the heroes in the story were not the powerful but the weak.

I thank the Lord for Melissa, and for her reminder to me through her simple prayer of these pictures of grace.

REST AND REFLECTION

Your Name

What fear might you have that keeps you from a deeper relationship with Jesus?

What areas of control get in the way of you trusting God?

SABBATH REST

Connie Lucille Peachey

"Remember to observe the Sabbath day by keeping it holy. You have six days each week for your ordinary work, but the seventh day is a Sabbath day of rest dedicated to the LORD your God. On that day no one in your household may do any work. This includes you, your sons and daughters, your male and female servants, your livestock, and any foreigners living among you. For in six days the Lord made the heavens, the earth, the sea, and everything in them; but on the seventh day he rested. That is why the Lord blessed the Sabbath day and set it apart as holy" (Exod 20:8–11, NLT).

We didn't fully understand the impetus behind observing a Sabbath day of rest. We saw it as a 'guideline'; an Old Testament institution that didn't really apply to New Testament Christians, especially Gentile Christians. A good idea but not required.

The work is never done in pastoral ministry. By the time a pastor does get a day off, home/family projects have often been left at the bottom of the 'to do' list. So in a frenzy we fly through the things left undone for far too long. The day comes and goes with nary a moment's rest. The week looms before us as another unending sea of demands cries for our attention. So, like a ship plowing through the sea, we just keep moving from one opportunity for ministry to another. Taking a day off from the Lord's work does not sound very spiritual.

So it was that, after 27 years of marriage and ministry, we found ourselves unable to carry on the tasks any longer and had to step out for a year of healing and restoration. It took three months for us to finally give ourselves permission to not set our alarm to make sure we got up at a respectable time. Someone had once said to us, "If I found out my pastor and his wife slept till 10 am I would no longer have any respect for them." *It's all about what people think, right?!*

Coming through, and out of, burnout is a long process. First of all, you have to take yourself off the responsibility hook of looking after the needs of others, and look after your own needs. Then you have to acknowledge the things that led you to burn out. Matters of the soul are difficult to discern unless you take time and give God access to your soul.

God continues to bring more and more healing, even as we have stepped back into ministry. We give ourselves permission to put our own oxygen mask on before we try to care for those around us. We now set aside a day to do the needed tasks of caring for the physical needs of our home, vehicles, family, etc. Then we also set aside a Sabbath rest day where we refrain from doing anything we 'should' do and try to do only those things we 'get to' do—the things that are life-giving. We usually have a plan, even if the plan is to stay at home and nap. We ask the Holy Spirit what He thinks would be life-giving and refreshing for us. Sometimes it is going for a Starbucks where we can sit and sip our favourite coffees as "Tom and Connie Who?" Sometimes we go hiking, canoeing or biking. Sometimes we listen to our favourite preachers (other than Tom) on DVD or online, or take in dinner and a movie. The point is that we have a day set aside to rest in the presence of God.

"Then Jesus said to them, 'The Sabbath was made to meet the needs of people, and not people to meet the requirements of the Sabbath'" (Mark 2:27, NLT).

Sabbath is a gift from God, a time meant for refreshing of our souls, bodies, and spirits. It is a good thing, not a restriction. It is what God did after He created the world.

"On the seventh day God had finished his work of creation, so he rested from all his work. And God blessed the seventh day and declared it holy, because it was the day when he rested from all his work of creation" (Gen 2:2–3, NLT).

God set in motion the example of a work/rest rhythm. When we take a Sabbath rest, we are acknowledging our dependence on God. If we work through the whole week, could it be that we are suggesting we can do this ourselves? Or, though we would never say it out loud, do we perhaps think the world couldn't possibly get by without us for 24 hours? Do we believe that God will not be able to provide the needed income we will miss if we take a day off? Taking a Sabbath is an issue of trusting God to look after us.

Jesus invited His disciples to stop doing 'ministry' for a bit:

"Then, because so many people were coming and going that they did not even have a chance to eat, he said to them, 'Come with me by yourselves to a quiet place and get some rest'" (Mark 6:31).

Notice what He *didn't* say: "Oh good, the work is done; now we can rest."

Notice what He *did* say: "Come with Me…"

I bless you, in the name of Jesus, to enter into a place of rest with Him. What is keeping you from setting aside a day each week to refrain from those things that *must get done* and just be still in God's presence? Why not follow our Creator's example and rest? Not because you must, but because He did. He invites you to join Him.

BEING THE WIFE OF JOB

Deborah Carpenter

If I could have coffee with any Bible character, I would want to have coffee with Job's wife. I think she gets a bad rap after her less-than-shining moment of faith ("Curse God and die").

She had experienced incredible losses—her blessed children, her beautiful home, and even her security when her husband was sick almost to the point of death. If Job died, her life in middle eastern culture would never be the same. Being a widow was a stigma that would leave her vulnerable and very much alone.

I would hazard a guess that she was feeling profoundly disillusioned. Her entire life was crumbling before her eyes, and yet somehow her husband was lamenting in an ash heap but still praising God!

Who was God to her in that moment? Certainly not benevolent and good. More likely He seemed aloof and far off. If I were Job's wife, cursing Him would probably not be such a stretch. It might feel cathartic to yell at the top of my lungs (if I'm honest).

Note that God does not respond to her curse. He doesn't call her out. She isn't shamed by Almighty God. Her pronouncement is left as is in Scripture—no commentary is made. Readers have gasped in horror at her lack of faith but somehow agree with Job as to God's lack of character. Interestingly, God spends four chapters asking Job who he thinks he is because Job had claimed his own innocence and accused God of lacking justice!

God almost acts as if her outcry didn't even happen. As He restored Job, God also restored Job's wife with a double portion of all she had lost—even seven more children! I don't think that is insignificant. Her honest words did not disqualify her from God's restoration.

I also wonder how foolish or shameful she felt after those words were uttered. How remorseful and repentant did she feel? How humbled did she feel as she watched her family and wealth restored to her and Job?

God could have cut her off, but He treated her as if she had said nothing. I think God understands disillusionment! I wonder if He appreciates our honesty?

(Note: Job's wife didn't curse God. She told her husband that *he* should curse God and then die. Perhaps her pain was so palpable that the only release she could perceive was death.)

I AM WORKING

Lynda Blazina

I have three kids. From oldest to youngest, there are three and a half years separating them, so we had a busy household when they were little! My oldest daughter grew up believing that she was a second mom to her siblings. I didn't instill this thought; in fact, I often battled against it. I would ask her, "Who's the mom?" and make her point to me.

If you've read anything on birth order, she is a typical firstborn—follow the rules, black and white, read directions and books from cover to cover. She's now studying law and loves it! Everything is laid out. These are the rules. Follow them and you'll be fine.

I am not a first child. I am the baby of my family. For me, everything is in flux, and schedules (and pretty much everything else) are fluid. I have a creative personality on top of that so my mind is just a jumble of thoughts at all times. I'm a daydreamer, an artist; the complete opposite of my firstborn.

Most of the time, our differences serve us well in our relationship. Both of us appreciate the strengths of the other…except when we don't! Sometimes there is rub, but that is also normal.

One time when the kids were quite young—my oldest was about five—I walked into the room as she was getting after her younger siblings (for some perilous wrong, I'm sure). Once again, I said, "Honey, I am the mom!"

She responded, "Well…you should act like it then." This reply was not sarcastic or lippy, just stated as fact. I'm sure her thought pattern resembled "If you're not going to do something about what I see happening, then someone needs to, so I will." I thought something along the lines of "This little one may struggle with some control issues in her future." What I didn't think was that she would come by them honestly, and that she might have inherited some of those issues from her mom.

I never thought that I was someone who needed to be in control. I thought I was pretty easygoing and could roll with the punches of life pretty easily—the total opposite of this little one who lived in her first-childness. I thought this…until life went out of my control.

During a time when everything already seemed to be turned upside down, one of my friends from high school passed away. Another friend had ended up being his pastor during his battle with cancer. I reconnected with him at the funeral.

As we were catching up, I relayed some of the struggles that my family had been walking through. I said something to the effect of "I never thought I was a control freak until lately, but now, with things out of my control, I don't like it very much!"

He responded, "Really? You, a control freak? I would never have guessed!" Unlike my daughter's, his response was both sarcastic and lippy, but it also stated a fact.

He quickly softened his reply by saying that he knew I had always liked things to look a certain way, to be presented properly, and to have everything together. People pictured me as strong, capable, and competent.

His response shook me. Those things don't mean I'm controlling, do they? Not always…but sometimes.

Life had been good to me up to that point, and I had come to believe that this was because of the way I lived and the decisions I made. Life had become a sweet place of enjoying the positive results of good decision making. I tried to be wise and to use good judgement, and that had positive payoff. This was not a bad thing, until my life became about controlling outcomes rather than enjoying the grace I had because of Jesus.

God brought me to a place of chaos so that I could acknowledge that, much like my oldest child, I was saying to my heavenly Father, "Well…You should act like it then."

When things were not turning out the way I would have liked or seen fit, I often would step in and try to be 'the God' of my circumstances. I found myself with the same attitude that my five-year-old had displayed: "Why aren't You doing anything about this?" His response was "I AM."

The Holy Spirit gently led me on a path of realizing that the great I AM is always at work, even when it doesn't look like it to our little, finite, human hearts. We can point to Him as 'the God' and rest in the fact that we are His children.

FORGIVE AS HE FORGIVES

Charleen Raschke

Why is it that forgiving some people is so much easier than forgiving others? Is it connected to the amount of expectation you put on a person? Or could it be connected to the depth of hurt their offence caused?

Over the years I have recognized within myself a combination of factors. I've had to forgive some individuals over and over again, while with others, forgiveness was a simple act, done in a moment, and the issue would never torment me again. There was one offender in particular that I forgave without too much difficulty. I understood what he did because I understood what had happened to him in his past, and I realized that he was stuck in a cycle. He needed Jesus to break him out of it. I am not saying that I trusted him—I didn't! I am saying that I understood, and understanding helped me to forgive him.

Trusting, forgiving, understanding, and boundaries are all separate things that can be connected in some ways. Unpacking these elements can help us walk into forgiveness.

Forgiveness, for example, does not mean we put ourselves in the position to be hurt again and again. Though I realize there are times when we have no control over this, there are other times when we need to set healthy boundaries in place to keep ourselves safe.

"So above all, guard the affections of your heart,
for they affect all that you are.
Pay attention to the welfare of your innermost being,
for from there flows the wellspring of life" (Prov 4:23, TPT).

It is up to us to guard our hearts and to pay attention to the welfare of our innermost being. No one else does that for us. It is our job to protect our hearts. Having the insight to understand where a person has come from, or what may have happened to that person to cause them to hurt others, is not an excuse for their actions, but it has helped me personally to forgive.

Trust, on the other hand, has to be earned, especially if it has already been broken. Trusting is not the same as forgiving. Trusting needs to go hand in hand with wisdom. It is not wise to trust people who continue to hurt others.

The hardest situations for me to deal with have been those where I've needed to forgive the same person repeatedly. In these instances, the person continues to do or say hurtful things with no regard at all for what they have done. We have to take care of our own hearts, by setting up healthy boundaries. We have to forgive.

Unforgiveness will keep us chained to the person who hurt us. It will taint other parts of our lives. Unforgiveness is not an option for followers of Jesus. His command to us is always to forgive.

Because of how much we have been forgiven, it is always a requirement for us to respond by forgiving any and all offences against us. This is His way. It is not always easy. Often it's a process and it's a choice.

In the example Jesus Himself gave us of how to pray, He says this:

"Forgive us the wrongs we have done as we ourselves release forgiveness to those who have wronged us" (Matt 6:12, TPT).

"And when you pray, make sure you forgive the faults of others so that your Father in heaven will also forgive you. But if you withhold forgiveness from others, your Father withholds forgiveness from you" (Matt 6:14–15, TPT).

PEACE IN THE UNKNOWN

Bonnie Lee

I was sitting in the emergency room for the third time in two days. My husband had woken up on Christmas Eve, turned on a light, and instantly had a migraine. This is quite common. Not the emergency room, but the migraine. This one seemed worse than most, though. In our experience, if medications couldn't get control over the monster, he would be admitted to the hospital.

There, usually a special pill would end it. That wasn't the case this time. He got an intravenous 'cocktail' of about six different medications to try to stop the migraine. It didn't work. Twelve hours later he got another cocktail with the same result.

Christmas morning, the migraine was well out of control. My husband was no longer able to talk, and he could not move the right side of his body. He started to cry as he asked me with slurred speech to take him back to the hospital. My heart was breaking for him, at what he must have been feeling, knowing how helpless he was in that moment.

We waited in emergency a few minutes for the doctor. When he arrived, I knew what he was thinking. My husband had stroke symptoms. The doctor wanted to transfer him to the closest major city, about a half hour away. I was calm and controlled on the outside as the doctor made the arrangements, but inside I was a complete mess.

As we drove to the city, I tried to stay strong for my husband because I could tell that he was scared. If I broke down, it would be messy. We waited for what seemed like forever in yet another emergency room, this time for the neurologist. The doctor asked a million questions, and by this time it was impossible, even for me, to understand what my husband was saying. It had gotten worse. He was disoriented and tipsy as he tried to walk.

The doctor decided to admit him into the stroke ward, and to run tests to see what was going on. It was now four in the afternoon. I hadn't been home with the rest of my little family, including my four-year-old, all day. Thoughts ran together through my mind: I have to go home. I don't want to leave my husband in this state. He is confused. He doesn't completely understand where he is. Why am I leaving without him? I want to stay and offer comfort. I have to help him settle in and talk to the nurses, because he can't talk. He can't write. He has no way to communicate.

I walked through the corridors of the hospital sobbing, because I didn't know if I would ever see my husband again. Don't get me wrong, I was sure he would survive this. But with brain injuries, you just don't know if personality and function will be completely restored. I cried out to God to be with him, because I couldn't, and I pleaded with Him to restore and heal.

I felt so hollowed-out and empty as I headed home alone. This man had become the most important person in the world to me. I couldn't imagine my life without him. I didn't want to imagine life without him. He was good and kind and loved God with his whole being.

I spent the next few hours with the rest of my family, then started calling my husband's family and more of mine and asking them to pray. That was literally the only thing we could do. I felt completely helpless in that moment.

The next day, new doctors came in. And the next day, more. This pattern continued for a week, until finally a young doctor gave me a diagnosis. It wasn't a death sentence, but it still felt hopeless. "Yes, this will happen again … No, we don't know if full function will be regained."

But in the midst of that diagnosis, the strangest thing happened in me. I felt God's peace. Completely. There is no way to explain the peace. I should have been devastated. I should have been falling apart. Yet there was peace—the peace of God. I had never in my life felt a peace that quite literally "passes understanding," as Philippians 4:7 says: "And the peace of God, which surpasses all understanding, will guard your hearts and minds in Christ Jesus."

Five weeks later, my husband *walked* into our home. As I write this, he is still recovering. He is still in therapy to help with some of the deficits from the stroke-like migraine that he had. He is still good and kind and in almost every way has been restored to the man he was before. He still loves God with his whole being.

Some days, thinking about what the future could hold terrifies me. Lately though, I find myself letting go of my preconceived ideas of where I thought God was leading, and of where I wanted to be at this moment in my life. I'm letting go of the fact that I have no control over my future. It's not that I don't trust God to finish what He started, but I find myself reflecting more on what I have in this moment.

My husband is home and well and healthy. I don't know what is going to happen tomorrow or the next day, but I have so many things to be thankful for in this moment—things I never knew I could thank God for. In the dust that settled after my husband's illness, I found myself thankful. Not for the illness, but for the strength God gave me through this ordeal and for the amazing peace that He granted to me day by day during the really hard times.

SEA OF WORSHIP

Lynda Blazina

A fog of elusiveness
covers my mind as I ponder
the meaning of 'worship':
The misty covering lifts.
Suddenly I see
or more, feel
an ocean of God's presence
surrounding and enfolding me.

The beauty of the sea is staggering,
like aqua cut crystal
yet liquid and filled with warmth.
Comfort that I can't quite describe.
Beckoning and compelling me to sink deeper.

As I peer up, I see what appears to be small rocks,
skittering across the crystalline surface of this deep.
With each skip,
I hear sweet songs being played and sung.

Then,
with a sudden splash
that interrupts the melodious comfort,

a large rock breaks the surface,
and floats down,
down,
down.
I notice this rock holds images and characters
of a certain type of drama.
I lean toward the stone and see a mom and dad.
They are hearing crushing news of their oldest son.
A beautiful teenage boy,
full of fun and vigour.
This boy,
whose life seems so full and endless,
now shows signs of brokenness revealed.
Ugly disease,
ravaging his blood and bones,
turning expectancy of life to death.
As the tender dreams they hold
are slowly and painfully shattered,
they bow in submission before a Holy Throne.
They choose hope,
not in medical miracles or chance remissions,
but in grace purchased through holiness,
poured out on a tree.
This hope is neither light nor hazy,
that comes then fades like a frozen breath—
This hope does not come naturally or easily,
yet they pursue it
and hold on
like a life-preserving anchor.

This:
is worship.

Another splash startles me,
and I look up again
to see another rock,
the same size as the first,
floating down into the depths of this unusual sea.
On this one,
I see the faces of three women,
Two daughters and a mom.
They are visiting a prison.
Across from them,
in this cold and unforgiving cage,
sits a broken and hurting man.
Tears are falling from his cheeks.
The women have every right to be angry
and condemning,
and live in the cold brought about through victimization.
This man
is accused of manslaughter.
In a stupor of self-medication,
he cut short a life…
the life of their husband and father.
Steeped in bitterness would seem allowable,
but instead
they lean over
and take the hands of the broken,
following the example of grace set out for them
by their Saviour and Comforter.
The only words they utter to this fellow sinner are
"We forgive you" and
"We love you as Christ loved us."

This:
is worship.

My heart is heavy seeing and sharing
in the hurt and pain of these stories.

Another splash above,
another rock falls through the deep
after shattering the musical and glassy surface.
On this one,
a father.
Up wandering the empty halls of his home,
his heart heavy for a wayward son.
A boy he bounced on his knee,
with blond curls and indigo eyes.
He feels the weight of guilt,
knowing not all his choices
were to this child's benefit.
Too many hours poured out into the lives of others,
instead of with this one that God entrusted to him.
He feels the loss of time.
His soul bleeds for the child whose own deep wounds
pushed him toward finding answers and comfort
in things not designed for him.
The dad bows his head.
His heart groans prayers of fear, doubt, guilt and repentance
upon the foot of a grace-covered cross.

This:
is worship.

More and more rocks fall.
Some with stories of forgiveness
in the face of injustice.
Some with pictures of grace undeserved.
All of them with the indelible markings of God's fingerprints,
as He shaped His character into lives.

I look down to the bottom of the ocean,
where the rocks have been falling.
and see a beautiful altar that they have formed.
I hear music with notes unknown to my ears,
yet they resound in my heart and soul.
Across the altar,
I see the words inscribed:
"Every knee shall bow,
Every tongue confess,
That Jesus Christ is Lord."

This:
is worship.

— DAY 63 —

REST AND REFLECTION

Your Name

Take a moment this week to write out some things that Scripture tells you about God's faithfulness and love for you.

If you need help, turn to Psalm 139.

KEEP YOUR EYES ON JESUS

Connie Lucille Peachey

I was looking for something encouraging to read. After turning to the front of my Bible and browsing the list of various topics, "Courage and Faith" seemed a good place to start. I was led to Hebrews 11. The context of this passage is the testimonies of the great men and women of faith in the Bible. Then it moves to God's discipline, which proves His love for His kids. Then I kept reading, and reading…

All the distress I have experienced and am still experiencing will be more than worth it in the end. The point of this passage seems to be "Keep your eyes on Jesus," no matter what. The people from the so-called Hall of Faith never got to see the promise fulfilled, yet they kept their eyes on the LORD. I am living in the promise. I also choose to keep my eyes on the LORD.

Imagine Noah, building the ark on an open plain with no water in sight. Oh, the ridicule. Or Abram, picking up all his worldly possessions and moving to an unknown land. What was he thinking? What did his family and friends think? And Sarah, giving birth to a little boy when she was too old and had been barren all her life. Not my idea of fun!

"All these faithful ones died without receiving what God had promised them, but they saw it all from a distance and welcomed the promises of God" (Heb 11:13, NLT).

Joseph, when he was dying, made his family promise to take his bones with them when they left Egypt. He knew God would bring his people out of Egypt one day. Walking through the Red Sea—on the ground that had been under the sea just minutes before—must have been terrifying, yet they did it and saw their Deliverer in action. Then a generation later, marching around the city of Jericho with its impenetrable walls… Day. After. Day. How silly! But on the seventh day, after the seventh time around the walls… *Wow*, that must have been something! Obviously, El Shaddai, the Almighty One of Jacob, was fighting for His people.

In Hebrews 11 we read of others who "trusted God and were tortured, preferring to die rather than turn from God and be free." Some were mocked, and their backs were cut open with whips. Some died by stoning, and some were cut in half (Heb 11:36–39).

The writer concludes this sobering chapter: "All of these people received God's approval because of their faith, yet none of them received all that God had promised" (Heb 11:39b, NLT).

They did not receive all that God had promised… not in this life.

But because of their testimony to us, in Hebrews 12:1–2, we are encouraged to "run with endurance the race that God has set before us." We do this by keeping our eyes on Jesus, on whom our faith depends from start to finish.

God, why is this happening to me, especially when I have served you with such fervour and devotion? When I have given up everything to follow you? I don't understand.

"Think about all my Son endured so He could purchase your freedom. He had the strength to walk the path to the cross because He knew what was in store. Joy." (See Heb 12:2.)

It's not only about a *someday* promise but about living in His presence *today*. Every one of the folks in the Hall of Faith had a personal encounter with the Living God. So, while they did not see the end result of the promise (Abraham did not see his descendants as numerous as the grains of sand; Joseph did not see the deliverance of his people from Egypt), they did experience God. They all walked with God on this earth in real time in the midst of some pretty tough situations.

I have seen my Deliverer, Provider, Protector, Redeemer, Healer, Comforter—and the list goes on—in action too. Life on this side of heaven may never be easy. It may never be without pain, sorrow, or grief. But I am walking daily in His presence. And one day, ONE DAY, I will be with Jesus forever! Then all the troubles of this world will be behind me.

"So take a new grip with your tired hands and stand firm on your shaky legs" (Heb 12:12, NLT).

Jesus is right there by your side! Just keep walking. Keep your eyes on Jesus.

HARD TO LOVE

Brenda Goudy

"**I** have loved you with an everlasting love. I have drawn you with unfailing kindness" (Jer 33:3).

"But because of His great love for us, God, who is rich in mercy made us alive with Christ even when we were dead in our transgressions—it is by grace you have been saved" (Eph 2:4–5).

"Brenda, you are easy to like, but hard to love."

Those words were spoken to me by an influential person in my life at a formative time, and have become a repeating voice in my head ever since. I'm sure that person didn't mean to hurt or impact me so deeply. Maybe the words were said in the heat of dealing with a frustrating adolescent attitude, or flippantly in an offhand comment. I have no recollection of the context. I only remember that I, and apparently who I am as my true self, am easy to like, but hard to love.

The interpretation my young, developing mind formed was that people would like me at first. I make a good first impression. However, if someone were to truly get to know me, or if I dared to let my guard down, I was not lovable. I believed that to be true. Unconditional love was not meant for me.

I lived my life trying to be fun, generous, and caring. I wanted to be likable and easy to be around. While I made new friends quickly, I never had any that lasted beyond a couple of years as my family moved every few years while I was growing up.

Over the past few years I have been challenged to search for truth in this area, and I have come to know that my identity is in Christ and in who He says I am. I am His daughter and He says I'm easy to love. He has used other people to challenge my deep-seeded beliefs about myself, and to embrace my value and worth in who I am in Christ and how He sees me.

Very early in my separation, a friend of mine was getting married in Mexico. I was extremely happy for her and excited for her destination wedding. Attending was not something that even crossed my mind.

Her parents were local pastors and had also been good friends of mine for years. A few weeks before the wedding, they contacted me and said a woman from their church wanted to meet with me and had something for me. All they said was that she had faced similar circumstances to mine when she was young, and that she had heard of my situation and felt empathy for me.

I thought this was kind of odd but sweet and I agreed to meet this lady, maybe to share stories and receive some words of encouragement from her. When I arrived at our friends' home I met a lovely older lady with kindness written all over her face. As I sat down and started drinking my coffee, I could tell something bigger was in the air. My friend prompted her to say something and, with tears in her eyes, she pulled out a small wooden box.

She explained that she had very little money but had taken an extra job recently and wanted to use her tithe from it to bless someone, rather than her usual giving to her church. She had talked with my friends (her pastors) and they suggested using it to send me to the wedding, so that I could enjoy being a part of it and get some much-needed rest and time away from all the stressors in my life.

I opened the box, and in it was enough cash to completely pay for the trip! I was overcome with emotion and gratitude, and she was as well. It truly was a full-circle moment for her, I believe, as she was able to pay forward and bless someone going through a hard time.

However, God wasn't quite done blessing me, or reminding me that He saw me, remembered me, and was guiding this blessing all along. When it was time to leave, I thanked her again and gave her a hug, and she whispered in my ear, "You're easy to love." My heart stopped. There was no reason for her to choose that phrase, or to use those words. I knew in that moment that God had put those exact words on her heart to speak to my soul. This wasn't just about a trip, or going to a wedding. It wasn't even about getting some much-needed rest and sun. It was about my Father reminding me of the truth, and using a complete stranger to speak it over me.

What words have people spoken over your life that have been given too much authority? We all have experiences with hurts and believing lies that the enemy plants in our minds. When those unwelcome thoughts come up, remember to turn your thoughts to the one who made you, who loved you enough to send His Son to die so that you could live forever with Him. Let's choose to believe who He says we are:

His daughter
Worthy
Created for a purpose
Valued
Cherished
Forgiven
Enough
Easy to like and…
…Easy to *love*.

THE GOD WHO IS ABLE

Lynda Blazina

Have you ever read a novel with such an intense story line that you just had to look ahead to make sure of the outcome before you continued reading? I have. It usually happens when I get so attached to a character that I just have to see if they survive against whatever great peril they are facing. I flip to some pages close to the back of the book and scan my eyes across a few paragraphs to see if their name is there. I don't want to wreck the adventure, just set my mind at ease.

But I have to admit, this takes the thrill out of the story. There are still pieces of the puzzle to discover, but I've cut down the climax of the story.

Too often when we read Scripture we do much the same thing. We've become familiar with the stories, so we read through them knowing the ending. We skip to the end where the lesson is—where God triumphs and blesses and carries His people through. However, there is much to gain by reading and meditating on the building blocks, the often-forgotten middle part, of the story.

We often read stories like that of Daniel and the lions' den, knowing that God stepped in and saved the day by sealing the lions' mouths. How often do we read that story and ponder the fact that Daniel didn't know that the Lord would save him? He was obedient to God in the face of great trial. His coworkers had such venomous hatred toward him that they worked to have the king form a law just to entrap Daniel with penalty of death.

Can you imagine the stress, anguish and trepidation that he must have felt in those days, knowing his obedience could cost him his life? Can you imagine the feelings of betrayal and frustration he must have felt toward his coworkers for their blind jealousy? The Bible describes Daniel as a man of great ability, faithful, always responsible, and completely trustworthy. I don't know about you, but I would have been questioning why God would let this happen to me. Wasn't Daniel doing life the way he had been taught and led to? Wasn't he exhibiting all the godly character that should shelter him from the consequences of living in a sinful world?

This was not Daniel's first run-in with surreal and unimaginable challenges either! The chapters of Daniel leading up to the lions' den are chapters laced with supernatural happenings. We see Daniel confronting kings, interpreting dreams, and refusing to bow down to an idol. He faced death, imprisonment, and watching his friends Shadrach, Meshach, and Abednego being thrown into an incinerator.

You would expect him at some point to throw up his hands and say, "Enough, Lord!" But he didn't. Why?

I think the key to this question is found in his friends' response to the king when they were about to be thrown into a furnace to be killed.

They responded to the king's declaration of "bow down to this idol or be put to death" by declaring:

"If we are thrown into the blazing furnace, the God whom we serve is able to save us. He will rescue us from your power, Your Majesty. But even if he doesn't, we want to make it clear to you, Your Majesty, that we will never serve your gods or worship the gold statue you have set up" (Dan 3:17–18).

Shadrach, Meshach, and Abednego didn't miss or skip over the climax of their story. They had seen the Lord perform miracles, and believed that He would save them. They stated this fact to the king. To us, it seems at first appearance that God saving their lives by stepping into the fiery furnace with them forms the pinnacle of the drama that was being played out in this story. In fact, this is just the finishing piece of the puzzle—the piece that makes the whole picture become clear and complete.

The climax of this account comes in Shadrach, Meshach, and Abednego's full statement to the king before God actually steps in and saves them. These three men had processed their situation and declared to the king who held their fate in his hands, "If we are thrown into the blazing furnace, the God whom we serve is able to save us" (Dan 3:17).

In the midst of great trial, these men had come to the conclusion that their hope was found in obeying and honouring God. Their hope did not come from whether or not they would be saved from their circumstances, it came from the fact that they worshipped the God who was able. They had seen the Lord perform miracles and believed that He would save them, but they chose to obey whether or not He did. They knew that God would be glorified through their obedience, and they left the particulars of how He would be glorified entirely up to God.

When we have the type of faith that allows us to worship the God who is able, whether or not He chooses to work in the way we would deem best becomes secondary, and our perspective regarding His activity within our personal situation changes.

This is the type of faith we are called to have—a faith in our God and in the amazing things that He can and will do through our lives and our stories, no matter how dire the situation. This gives us hope, not because our situations will necessarily be reconciled according to what we perceive as *good*, but in our knowledge of and faith in the character of God.

Faith in God simply because He is able compels us toward both worship and obedience in spite of our circumstances. We are then able to place our circumstances into His hands and become observers of God being glorified through our stories.

BURNING HEARTS AND BREAKING BREAD

Deborah Carpenter

In the days after my husband's accident, and then again in the days after my brother's death, my kitchen was filled with food. Fruit basket upon bread basket, casserole upon casserole, and lots and lots of baking. Those who dropped their provisions off rarely stayed, content in knowing they had blessed us with the gift of comfort food. Some came by to visit, gifting us with their own tears and presence. We could bring out a casserole and share a meal. Even though my taste buds refused to tell me if I liked the food, my body was grateful for the nourishment. My soul was, too. In the fellowship of these believers, my eyes and heart were opened to the promise and comfort of God's presence.

I remember a story from 2,000 years ago about another shared meal after the death of a very good friend. It was the meal shared in Emmaus between two friends and one stranger. This story has a surprise twist.

"While they were talking and discussing together, Jesus himself drew near and went with them. But their eyes were kept from recognizing him. And he said to them, 'What is this conversation that you are holding with each other as you walk?' And they stood still, looking sad… When he was at table with them, he took the bread and blessed and broke it and gave it to them. And their eyes were opened, and they recognized him. And he vanished from their sight.

"They said to each other, 'Did not our hearts burn within us while he talked to us on the road, while he opened to us the Scriptures?' And they rose that same hour and returned to Jerusalem. And they found the eleven and those who were with them gathered together, saying, 'The Lord has risen indeed, and has appeared to Simon!' Then they told what had happened on the road, and how he was known to them in the breaking of the bread" (Luke 24:15–35, ESV).

Note a couple of things from this passage.

Amid their sadness, Jesus Himself draws near. But He keeps His real identity hidden from them. I have no real answer for why He chose to do so, but I like to think of it as an example of how Jesus is not afraid of us in our grief and our sadness. Instead He enters it with us.

In this passage, Jesus asks what is wrong and then listens carefully to the story of the two men, waiting until they are done before speaking the truth to them. Even His admonishment for their slow hearts is followed by the greatest encouragement I can think of—a walk through the entirety of Scripture, showing how the prophecy of the Messiah had been fulfilled in the life and death of Jesus, all the while never revealing that He, that same Messiah, was alive and walking with them.

It wasn't until they were "breaking bread" together that their eyes were opened, perhaps because they had seen it done before…at the last meal they had…with Jesus.

Oh, what joy to realize that the women were indeed telling them the truth when they announced that Jesus was alive! What joy to know that they had not put their hope of the Messiah in the wrong man; that they had just spent hours with Him in conversation and fellowship. Their hearts had "burned within them," so powerful was His presence. When Jesus finds us, regardless of whether we recognize Him or not, our spirits know. Not in the moment perhaps, but we know.

Once they knew who Jesus was, the men rose up that same hour and headed back to Jerusalem to tell the others. Their experience with Jesus was so powerful and exciting that it compelled them to race back to the other disciples and share their story. In doing so, they did for the disciples what Jesus had just done for them: entered their sadness and gave them a reason to rejoice.

TRUST OR CONTROL?

Charleen Raschke

"Trust in the Lord completely, and do not rely on your own opinions. With all your heart rely on him to guide you, and he will lead you in every decision you make" (Prov 3:5, TPT).

I sometimes wonder if I will be learning for the rest of my life just how out of control I really am. Life has a tendency to throw us curve balls without warning most of the time. Less-than-ideal situations come right out of left field. Sexual abuse, a parent's addiction, poverty, bullying, a child born with disabilities, sexual assault of a child, a child who ends up an addict living on the streets, a child arrested and in prison, the death of a family member, excruciating physical pain...just to mention a few things I've personally lived through.

If it were up to me—if I could really control the things that come my way—I would have planned a much safer, healthier, cushier existence, believe me!

The reality is that none of us can control the things we often find ourselves dealing with. In real life we have to learn how to navigate the difficult and painful events we have been handed. I have never been a fan of pain and I'm guessing neither have you. I mean, I'm grateful for the response my body gives me, reminding me that I'm still alive (the one way in which pain is actually a gift), but I would really prefer never to have any, ever!

So, what can we control? I have learned that I can control my responses to the things that happen to me and to my family. I can make the effort to pursue Jesus and the healing He offers to my broken heart. No one else has the ability to control this.

Control can look a lot like 'helping' or 'rescuing.' If I am constantly trying to shield someone I care about from a consequence they need to feel, I am trying too hard to control things. That is not our job.

Those of us who have had alcoholic parents, or who have been sexually abused, often feel the need to control our circumstances. We have felt so out of control for so long that, unless we pursue inner healing, we will find ourselves in this control cycle over and over again.

I have learned over the years that I cannot control my husband, my kids, my friends, or my relatives. (And yes, I have tried!) But I can reach out to them, and I can love them.

This is where I have learned to exchange control with trust. I have to trust Jesus with the ones I love. I have to trust that He loves them even more than I do. And I have to trust that He cares far more than I do.

It is this trust that actually replaces the former control with a peace that goes deep.

CHANGING OF SEASONS

Lisa Clarke

I have experienced many different seasons in my life. Winter always leaves me longing. Longing for new growth, longing for thawing…just longing.

I love the carefree days of summer when I can visit the beach and praise God for warmth. As spring turns into summer and then to fall, I have learned that winters allow me time to slow down in certain areas in my life. I have met some people who love winter! They love winter sports and sitting down to a hot drink in front of the fire.

The spiritual season of winter can seem cold, long, and empty. We know that we will all go through these seasons of winter, and as I reflect on the different seasons in my life, surprisingly, or maybe not, winter has often been the most profound.

In seasons of winter, I have been thankful that Scripture has been there to turn to. Recently, I have been studying Romans and Revelation. Throughout Romans, we are reminded of so many truths that are like that hot drink by the fire, such as the truth that, by Christ's finished work on the cross, we are justified. Romans 8 says that the Spirit intercedes for us and that this is God's love displayed. It also says that Jesus never leaves us and that there is no condemnation for those in Christ Jesus.

Romans encourages us that, no matter what we face in this life— trials, persecutions, troubles—"no height, nor depth…can separate us from the love that is in Christ Jesus" (8:37). Romans 11 brings this all to a crescendo with a doxology about God's mercy to all.

Along with Romans, the book of Revelation has also been opening up to me. As I read through Revelation, I find so many more warm embers of truth for this cold season, but the one that I keep coming back to is the glorious fact that God provided everything for free. Revelation 21:1–7 states that Christ is the Beginning and the End, and that everyone can come without cost to the living water forever. That is our victory and ultimately our home, with Christ in the new heavens and new earth.

In my distinct seasons of winter, I remind myself of this victory often. Sometimes the wait feels so long. Days drag on and there seems to be no end in sight. Yet, as Romans and Revelation remind us, God is with us and new seasons are coming.

I will end with this encouragement from Hosea 6:3:

"Let us acknowledge the LORD; let us press on to acknowledge him. As surely as the sun rises, he will appear; he will come to us like the winter rains, like the spring rains that water the earth."

REST AND REFLECTION

Your Name

There is a lot of talk these days about self-care.

What are some of the ways you care for your soul?

What does your soul need?

What do you do to attend to the needs of your soul?

How has God cared not only for you, but for your soul?

STEPPING OUT

Ryshon Blazina

Isaiah 43 says: "Fear not, for I have redeemed you; I have called you by name, you are mine. When you pass through the waters, I will be with you; and when you pass through the rivers, they will not sweep over you. When you walk through the fire, you will not be burned; the flames will not set you ablaze" (vv. 1–2, ESV.)

"Forget the former things; do not dwell on the past. See, I am doing a new thing! Now it springs up; do you not receive it? I am making a way in the wilderness and streams in the wasteland" (vv. 18–20).

You will never step into God's plan and destiny for your life if you are too stuck in your own issues. Now, before you get mad at me, know that I understand that life is hard.

Sometimes things are so difficult that there really is no way out but for the love of the Father, and walking through grief and hurt looks different and takes a different amount of time for everyone.

However, I believe it is also a huge tactic of the enemy to keep you in a place of hurt; to keep you out of God's plan for your freedom and calling on your life.

To be focused on Jesus, we have to sacrifice being focused on the past. Things you have been through or are going through are all on purpose, for a purpose.

In your circumstances that seem desolate and hopeless and dry, He is working for *good* to produce a new glory in you. Sometimes staying in a place of grief is a lot easier than trying to step forward into peace, and into dreams and purpose, but there is always freedom found in Jesus. Try taking a step out of hurt. Trust in the one who takes disappointment and hurt and uses it for our benefit.

— DAY 72 —

THE WILL OF GOD

Connie Lucille Peachey

"'Don't be afraid,' Samuel reassured them. 'You have certainly done wrong, but make sure now that you worship the LORD with all your heart, and don't turn your back on him'" (1 Sam 12:20, NLT).

"The Lord will not abandon his people, because that would dishonor his great name. For it has pleased the LORD to make you his very own people" (1 Sam 12:22, NLT).

What happens when we disobey God? When He has asked us to do something and we blatantly go another direction? Is there a one and only will of God that destines us to be hooped forever and live a second-best life if we miss it? Is it possible to relegate ourselves to a life of concessions rather than God's best plans?

The context for the above verses is that Israel wanted to be like the nations around them and have their own visible, physical king. God was their king, but they wanted a 'real' one. So Samuel, following God's direction, anoints Saul as their king. As Samuel recounts God's faithfulness to his people they are hit with the awareness that they have offended God with their request for a king. They repent. God forgives them. God gives them a king anyway. His desire is to be at the centre of their hearts, with or without a human king.

God does that in our lives too. He may have wanted us to turn right, but we turned left. When we repent we must sometimes continue on that left-turn path because it has been set and cannot be changed. What does change is that we begin walking *with* God instead of walking *away* from Him. It is not the destination, or even how we arrive at said destination, that is the main thing. It is God's desire, His will, that we walk with Him.

God's best plan is to have a relationship with us. He has gone to extreme lengths to make that possible.

"This is how much God loved the world: He gave his Son, his one and only Son. And this is why: so that no one need be destroyed; by believing in him, anyone can have a whole and lasting life. God didn't go to all the trouble of sending his Son merely to point an accusing finger, telling the world how bad it was. He came to help, to put the world right again" (John 3:16–17, MSG).

I have listened to the stories of many people who have the idea that God is watching from above, waiting for us to mess up so He can fling His judgement down on us. Or, at the very least, He is so disappointed with us when we get it wrong that He gives us the silent treatment—folding His arms across His chest, pouting, as He turns His face away. Many people believe there is nothing we can do to please this tyrant Father, and when we do make a wrong choice we are doomed to live with the consequences for the rest of our lives. This is not the God who sent His Son to pay for all the wrong in the world.

Many people equate consequences with disfavour. My six-year-old grandson was jumping in a bouncy house one day. As he was about to come out my daughter told him, "Do not jump down from there! Let me help you." He was tough. He could handle the jump. So, disregarding his mother's command, he jumped. His jump was not executed as he had anticipated and he landed on his shoulder, snapping his collar bone. He screamed in pain and was instantly repentant.

The pain did not stop the moment he repented. The collar bone had to be set and he had to wear a sling for a few weeks. The reminder of his disobedience was with him for quite some time. Did his mother stop loving him because he had disobeyed? Of course not. Did she stop feeding him and clothing him to show him that disobedience was not to be tolerated? Of course not. She loved him. She cared for him. She even did some chores for him that he was not able to do until his collar bone healed. He suffered the consequences of not obeying his mother's will for several weeks, but his mother never stopped loving him. He remained in relationship with her.

"The LORD appeared to us in the past, saying: 'I have loved you with an everlasting love; I have drawn you with unfailing kindness'" (Jer 31:3).

God is not nearly as concerned with our behaviour as He is with our heart. His will is that we live in relationship with Him. Read John 3:16–17 again, this time with your name in the blanks:

"This is how much God loved_____: He gave His Son, His one and only Son. And this is why: so that no one, not even_____, need be destroyed; by believing in Him, _____can have a whole and lasting life. God didn't go to all the trouble of sending His Son merely to point an accusing finger, telling _____ how bad _____ was. He came to help, to put _____'s world right again."

Jesus wants to make your world—your inner world—right again. There is nothing you can do to disqualify yourself from His love. I invite you to give Him your heart and step into relationship with Him.

HOPE FOR
THE LEFT BEHIND

Kerry Robideau

"For we walk by faith, not by sight—we are of good courage, I say, and prefer rather to be absent from the body and to be at home with the Lord" (2 Cor 5:7–8, NAS).

It was 2001 when I received a phone call from my mom. "Kerry, I know you have enough on your plate, but I have to tell you that I have cancer." It was devastating. My father-in-law, his skin grey and pale, had been sitting in ICU for six months waiting for a heart transplant. We would make the drive to the University of Alberta hospital as often as we could to support him and my mother-in-law, not knowing how long he would have to live. Now it was my mom. She was diagnosed with stage three ovarian cancer in November of that year, and on Christmas Eve she had surgery to remove as much of the cancer as the surgeon could take.

Christmas was one of my mom's favourite holiday celebrations. She always made sure we were thoroughly spoiled and had fun in the process. This Christmas was somber for us. My dad, my husband, our three children, and my brother and sister-in-law gathered in our home for breakfast, opened gifts, and then headed to the Royal Alex hospital to be with Mom, awaiting the prognosis from the doctor after the surgery. The surgical team had not been able to take the entire tumour from where it had attached itself to the bottom of the abdominal wall, which meant there were still cancer cells in her system. Not knowing what was going to happen next, she was released from hospital after a couple of weeks of healing and, a few months later, the chemotherapy treatments began. She had six treatments and, despite the 'seedlings' of cancer still in her other organs, the cancer went into remission. There was hope that life, her life and ours, would return to some normalcy.

Just short of two years later (the time required in remission to be considered cancer-free), I received another phone call. "Kerry, the cancer is back." This time it was worse, stage four. The 'seedlings' had grown and spread to her lungs and intestines. A choice had to be made between letting the cancer take its course or trying another, more aggressive form of chemotherapy that would take any quality of life she might have left and couldn't guarantee any quantity. As she explained it all to me, I responded with tears in my eyes, "Mom, you don't have to do this [chemotherapy] for us. It's okay." We sat in silence for a moment, and then she thanked me.

I wasn't sure I was ready to lose my mom. We were very close. She was an anchor in my life, a confidante, an encourager and support in prayer, but God was asking me to let her go. He wanted her home with Him. What choice did I have? I did have my moments of anger, wondering why He would take her from us. He must have known that we still needed her.

As guilty as she felt at times about leaving us behind, truly her desire was to be with Jesus. On September 26, 2005 at 3 am, Mom left to be with the Lover of her soul.

Some hard lessons were learned during those four years. Life isn't always fair, and God is supreme. It's not easy to understand why God does or doesn't do certain things for us or for those we love. For some reason those understandings are reserved for heaven. I saw how strong Mom's faith was, how courageous and peaceful she was in the midst of her own pain. I wanted that in my life, and it encouraged me to respond the same way in the midst of my own pain at that moment.

I learned how strong I could be in faith and love. Loving someone deeply moves me to act courageously, to provide what is needed in the moment without hesitation.

Her leaving has put in my heart a greater longing for heaven, and for the day I will see her again with Jesus. Where I depended on her for prayer and encouragement, I've had to rely on Jesus in a greater way. That dependence on Him has led to a deeper faith as I've watched Him meet my need for godly support and encouragement. Sometimes that was just between Him and me; other times He supplied flesh and blood.

Mom doesn't need hope anymore, for "faith is the assurance of things hoped for, the conviction of things not seen" (Heb 1:1). She stands where hope is fulfilled. For those of us left behind, our hope is in the one who knows the number of our days. As we "walk by faith, and not by sight," we do it all in the hope that there is Someone greater than ourselves who loves us deeply and has our best in mind. He fills our hearts with a longing for heaven, for something better than anything we could ever have on earth, and reminds us that there is no such thing as heaven on earth.

LOSING YOUR IDENTITY

Charleen Raschke

We had just come through the worst storm we had ever encountered. My role over the previous few years had been mainly caretaker and fighter for my family. I was the one who drove our daughter to her counselling sessions, so that she could one day experience freedom. I was the one who did all of the background work for our son's court day. I was the one who found that same son a safe haven for the next year of his life. I was also the one who continued to deal with our other son's daily special needs and help him, including dealing with every issue and phone call we received from his school.

Though there were many times I longed for things to ease up, I knew my place and found tremendous purpose in it. After all, I was needed by everyone in my family.

Then shifts began to happen. My daughter got healthier, and was also transitioning into being an adult. My older son was also getting healthier as he completed a year of rehab and began his year of house arrest. My husband and I were still reeling from all of the pain and stress that had compounded over the years. We were both obviously battered by the storms, but in the horrific times we had just passed through, I had had purpose. I was the mom. I was the one who would do anything to fight for the freedom and safety of my kids, and that was exactly what I had done.

I wasn't expecting what happened next. What should have been a natural transition became so incredibly painful that it literally knocked me to my knees.

Our daughter had turned 18. In her mind, that was it. She was an adult, and she began to make decisions that crushed her father and me. The tug-of-war for her independence was a brutal blow to us, mainly because of how she went about it. The sneaking around behind our backs was hard, but the day she came home and packed up her things, with no warning at all, was the blow that sent me on a downward spiral. I begged her not to go even as she walked out our front door, but it was to no avail.

As the door closed behind her, I felt like a red-hot poker had pierced my heart. I wept for days. What should have been a time of mother and daughter dreaming together and celebrating this milestone was ripped from us. One more blow.

I couldn't wrap my mind around it, probably because of the damage that had already been done to my heart. I mean, how could she no longer need me after all we had just walked through? If she didn't need me, then I didn't know where I belonged. What was my purpose? Who was I?

Identity: "character as to who a person is; the qualities, beliefs, etc., that distinguish or identify a person" (Dictionary.com, Nov 2018).

Because of how long the season of crisis had been, and how long I had been needed, my identity became fused with the feeling of being deeply needed. My family had experienced very real needs that were not the day-to-day norm. But to break out of the unhealthy connection I had made between my identity and being needed—to disentangle myself from that—hurt even more.

When a hurting person begins to walk in a healthy place, those who were once needed by that hurting person often struggle to celebrate. Relationships change in this transition, and they should! Shifts happen that need to happen.

My relationship with Jesus took a lot of hits over that period of time. While I never let go of Him entirely, much damage took place as I flailed in pain and disappointment.

It took a few years for me to find my place again. My misplaced identity needed to be realigned with the One whose I am. Through counselling and much prayer, I began to feel my feet underneath me once again. As I stepped forward, tiny step by tiny step, purpose came back into focus.

Ultimately, where I needed to go back to was intimacy with Jesus. I needed to spend time in His presence, listening for His voice. This is, after all, who I am. I am His. I am fully His!

Song of Songs 1:8 (TPT):
"Listen, my radiant one—if you ever lose sight of me,
just follow in my footsteps where I lead my lovers.
Come with your burdens and cares."

A SMALL, SMOOTH STONE

Lynda Blazina

I love beaches. They have held some significant moments of healing for me. There is something about hearing the consistent sound of the water lapping up on the sand, as it has since the beginning of time, that is therapeutic to my soul.

After a particularly tough season filled with many spiritual and emotional battles, my husband and I decided to pack up our little family and go on an extended holiday. Our month away included beaches along the California and Oregon coastline.

Walking along the shore with my bare feet in the sand, I picked up a small black rock. It was about the size of a flat walnut, and had been worn smooth by the persistent tides. As I looked at it, I thought of the story of David and Goliath in 1 Samuel. This story describes King Saul trying to prepare David for battle by covering him with his armour. But David, shedding the armour, picked out the stones that would finally kill the giant Goliath.

"David said to Saul, 'I'm not used to them.' So David took them off. Instead, he took his staff in his hand and chose five smooth stones from the wadi and put them in the pouch, in his shepherd's bag. Then, with his sling in his hand, he approached the Philistine" (1 Sam 17:39–40).

I looked down at the small, smooth stone in my hand. I had a hard time picturing myself as David, shedding the king's armour and picking up a little rock like this one instead.

In fact, as I thought about my life, I realized I had been gathering and stockpiling as much armour as I could. I didn't care if it was comfortable or fit me or felt natural. I didn't care if I could fight in it. There were giants looming, and I wanted enough armour. I wanted to bury myself under as much of the protective cover as I could find.

If I ever did pick up a stone, I don't think my natural inclination would have been to pick up a small, smooth one. Maybe a jagged one—one that looked as much like an arrowhead as possible, or one that seemed to have some weight to it!

But David knew that it wasn't really about the stones he picked up. He was walking in obedience, and in honour of the Lord's name. The Philistines were insulting more than just his country and threatening even more than the nation he loved. They were calling out against his God.

David knew that his protection, his true armour, had nothing to do with spears, swords, muscle, or brawn. His protection, his victory in the battle, was up to the Lord alone. He was so confident in this fact that when Goliath made an offensive attack against him, "David ran quickly to the battle line to meet the Philistine" (1 Sam 17:48)…

…with nothing but five small, smooth stones and his sling.

I often wonder why David didn't at least use a spear, a common weapon of the time. He was a shepherd and would have had some knowledge of and practice with a spear!

I believe the reason is that God wanted to use the ridiculous, the laughable, and the obvious lack on David's side of the battle to show *His* greatness in the victory!

Looking again at my life, I knew there were some victories that God wanted to win with stones. Little, smooth, common, everyday stones like loving my enemies, obedience, listening, prayer, kindness, and gentleness. These were things that where laughable and ridiculous in my own strength but, when put into a sling and directed by the Lord's hand, would fell the enemy and bring victory to His name.

I still have that little stone. It sits in my jewellery box as a reminder of the truth that my victory is in Jesus Christ, and nothing else. Not in my might, or power, or wisdom, or best thinking and arguments, but in the Spirit of the Lord. When He is for me, there is nothing that can stand against me.

THE JOURNEY OF TRANSFORMATION

Stefanie Carlson

"The two most important days of your life are the day you are born, and the day you realize why." — Mark Twain

I recently took a trip to Mexico City, where I joined an amazing team in the super-powered mission of ending human trafficking. It was during this trip that I found my purpose.

During our trip I was able to give haircuts to some everyday heroes who have overcome human slavery. I also had the opportunity to give a makeup class to some young survivors—shockingly young. Each one of them was courageously facing the pain of her trauma head on. I have never been more inspired and broken in all my life.

My realization of my purpose during those days made me want to celebrate the journey of transformation. These women have worked so hard on their inner healing, and I want to honour them by passing on some tools that may encourage a transformation in each of your lives as well.

The first step is connecting with *your* story. As Brené Brown so beautifully writes in her book *Rising Strong*, "Do we want to write the story or do we want to hand the power to someone else? Choosing to write our own story means getting uncomfortable; it's choosing courage over comfort."

I encourage each one of you to step out of your comfort zone and connect with your story. Shame may make an appearance, but that identity has no place in your life. Press through the ugliness and write down your story—a vulnerable unedited version of who you are and what you have overcome. Nobody needs to see this; it is just part of the process.

I have found that it helps to process the following after you've written out your story:

- What do you value? These things help you make decisions about how you will spend your time and resources.

- What is the vision you have for your life? What are the things that help you see where you want to go with your story and your life?

- What is the purpose that God has designed for you and your story?

Each one of you reading these words has a story full of destiny and purpose. We can all use our passions to change the world around us. This can happen in our own communities or on a grander scale, but first our eyes need to be opened to the possibility that God has placed inside each and every one of us.

Share your passion. You can be empowered by doing things for or by yourself, but you can be super-powered by doing things *with* others. Surround yourself with people who lift you up. Start following that Instagram account that makes you feel alive and inspired. Read more, meditate, and treat your body like the temple that it is.

Spend time with God. Let Him tell you who you are. Start asking Him what He sees in you and why He's given you the story He has.

"Before I formed you in the womb I knew you, before you were born I set you apart" (Jer 1:5a).

"Now you are the body of Christ, and each one of you is a part of it" (1 Cor 12:27).

REST AND REFLECTION

Your Name

What cares do you find yourself facing?

If God were to remove that care, how would things change?

Visualize Jesus in the flesh, sitting in your living room, asking you to cast your cares on Him.

What would you give Him to care for?

Does His physical presence change your willingness to leave those burdens with Him?

CARRIED BY HIS GRACE

Charleen Raschke

How often am I aware of God's grace in my life? Most of the time, to be completely honest, I just carry on with my life completely unaware! But every now and then, the Holy Spirit, for whatever reason, allows me to see at least a glimpse of His grace.

One of those times was after our daughter was raped. Our entire family was grieving and in an incredibly dark season. We were all going for counselling. Somewhere along that journey, the Holy Spirit, in His gentle way, showed me how kind He really was and is. Even in the midst of unbelievable pain. Even when I only had the strength to pray "Help." Even when I was unsure if there was hope left for us. He came and He allowed me to see just a tiny glimpse of how He, in His grace, had been preparing me for this. How He had made me ready to stand, not just for myself, but for my entire family.

How on earth could God have possibly been preparing me for a day, a time, when my family was so blown apart by pain? How was this even possible?

This is what He showed me:

For about a year before our daughter's assault, God had been working on me. He was using a gifted, prophetic counsellor named Heather. She was a gentle, Spirit-filled woman.

I initially went to her hoping she could 'fix' my husband. After all, he needed some fixing for sure! Seeing my attempt to control him, to manipulate him, really, she called me out. Actually, she asked me, "Have you ever been sexually abused?"

I think I must have had a bit of a stunned look on my face as I said "Yeah…," thinking, "What on earth does this have to do with my husband needing to smarten up?"

It actually had everything to do with it. Yes, I had been sexually abused as a young girl. And yes, it was affecting everything in my life. Mostly it was affecting my marriage. I was broken in so many ways and had learned to live from that broken place. Living in brokenness had become my normal.

I began counselling with Heather, week after week, until both she and I felt that a work had been completed in my heart. It took some time, but I really wanted to embrace the change and I wanted my heart to be healed.

This was the gift of grace that God was showing me. When our daughter told us what had happened to her, I knew instantly that this was the woman who would help my daughter like she had helped me.

Seeking out a godly, trustworthy, safe place to go with our daughter could have weighed heavily on us. But because God had allowed me to get wise and godly counsel, I knew where she could go for help, too.

What a gift of grace Heather was to all of us!

NOT MY STORY

Amy Cordell

"Bear one another's burdens, and so fulfill the law of Christ"
(Gal 6:2, ESV).
"He gives power to the weak and strength to the powerless"
(Isa 40:29, NLT).

Fear shivered down my spine as the counsellor at the women's shelter spoke. "So now I have to ask you. You mentioned you are a person of faith—do you belong to a church?" It had already taken all my energy to maintain some composure for the past hours, just as it had taken all my bravery to finally go to see a counsellor at the shelter.

"Yes," I replied warily. Was she going to report me to my pastor? Was she going to tell me that I had to stay with my husband and endure the treatment I had lived with for the sake of being a Christian? Nothing could have prepared me for what she said next.

"Then you need to prepare yourself to be rejected by them. Your husband will go there first and turn them against you. They will not support you, and will leave you isolated."

"No," I confidently replied, "My church family is supportive and knows and trusts me. I have attended there for over ten years and I know they won't leave me and my children unsupported."

"I'm so sorry to say this," her eyes were full of sympathy and I felt her sorrow for what would surely be a disappointment for me, "but I have seen it over and over again. Christians don't want to take sides, or they don't want to look as though they support divorce. I've seen so many women whose husbands have planted seeds of doubt against them and stolen away any support they should have received."

"That will not be my story," I confidently stated.

Days later, sitting in my lawyer's office, I was again shaking with fear of the unknown and trying to make sense of what was happening in my life. I was going to have to file for divorce, which was something I never wanted to have happen. I had to make decisions to protect and support my children and our future.

My confident, tough, yet kind lawyer said she was passionate about helping women in my situation. And as a Christian, she wanted to help other Christian women in my situation as best she could.

"I need to prepare you," she said to me, with the now-familiar sympathy in her eyes. "Your church will turn against you. People who you think are your friends, and who have promised to be there for you, will disappear. You need to be prepared for the rejection and find other sources of support."

"That will not be my story," I said again as confidently as I could after hours of exhausting discussion and planning the next steps I would need to take.

"I've seen it too often. In fact, I've never seen a church support a woman in your situation," she replied, just as confidently.

"That will not be my story," I repeated, more emphatically and with a growing sense of resolve to cling to my supports and only grow stronger no matter what came my way.

My counsellor and lawyer were right. My reputation was attacked relentlessly. Stories, lies and innuendos were thrown around like confetti.

However, I was also right. My church family surrounded us, believed and supported me, assured me over and over of their unconditional love, and also offered help and guidance to my husband. Many times he was asked to meet with church people for help, guidance and direction.

My experience was one of unconditional love. Church families offered a place to stay if my kids and I needed it. They shared where extra house keys could be found and ensured I knew that the offer was genuine. Others hid bags with pyjamas, toothbrushes, and changes of clothes in case they were needed in an emergency.

Friends committed to attending every meeting, court date and mediation session so I would never be alone. They drove me where I needed to go and stayed as long as I needed them to stay, even taking time off work and sitting in a waiting area for hours. These ladies promised to be my safety net to catch me if I fell. They were my anchors.

Still others spent hours going through papers looking for documents I needed. They made meals so I didn't have to cook and prepared lunches for my kids to take to school. Notes, cards, gifts, and words of encouragement would always arrive at just the time I needed them. My church provided food and help with school supplies, always with a word of support and encouragement so I didn't feel embarrassed. Friends even purchased a home so the kids and I could have affordable living space, within the boundaries of the kids' schools so they wouldn't have to switch.

In the toughest times, hearing the words "We believe you," "We stand with you," and "I will always be your friend" were lifelines that got me through. My church family was life in action and helped to bear my burdens.

I am proud to say that I was right. I'm also humbled to say that I was right. I have spoken to countless women who have escaped similar situations to mine, and none of them have my story. I often feel I do not deserve the blessing I was given in my church family. At the same time, I am ashamed that in some circles the reputation of the church is that they will turn their backs on women and children in threatening situations. The more I share my story, the more I pray and hope that this will change in our communities and that churches will take a stand in support of women in need. This is not to say that men don't need support, or that men are always at fault. My prayer is simply that the church will surround their families with love, and not be afraid to take action and honour God in the way they handle life's messy situations.

I know I will be less likely to judge and more active in supporting those who are hurting. I know the power that love has to bring hope when life seems hopeless. I pray that more churches will not be afraid to embrace and support women in need, so that more women sitting in shelters or lawyers' offices, being warned of rejection by their church families, can look them in the eye and confidently say, "That will not be my story."

SWIMMING IN CIRCUMSTANCES

Lynda Blazina

I was sitting in my living room enjoying a sudden little burst of 'normalcy' during a season of deep grief, loss and brokenness. I was beginning to sense that God really was at work in spite of a lot of really terrible circumstances.

Lately, I had been hearing some great sermons and felt like the Lord had been speaking right to me. I began to feel alive again and to trust that I served a God who cared and loved me and saw me in my need.

Then someone I loved came into my quiet little living room and …

Wham! … another chunk of devastating news that hit me from behind. Another circumstance I did not see coming.

Instantly, I started doubting everything. Was I living in spiritual delusion? Had I been hearing from the Lord? Was God actually at work or had I been spinning a fairy tale out of the few good circumstances I had recently encountered?

I remember, even in the reeling, hearing, "When are you going to trust Me?" It felt a lot like the words of Jesus after He met the disciples in the storm and Peter walked on the water…then sank: "You of little faith, why did you doubt?" (Matt 14:31).

I'm sure you've read the story. Raging wind. Rough waters. A boat being tossed to and fro. You've been there too, I'm sure. Days that rage with issues, problems, and negative circumstances. The feeling of being tossed to and fro in your emotional and spiritual life.

Before the storm hit in my living room that day, the Lord had been proving Himself over and over to me in the middle of my messes. He had shown Himself, He had whispered His name to me, and He had assured me of who He was.

Like Peter, I had begun to put my trust where it should be, on the capable shoulders of Jesus. Also like Peter, once I was out on the water and needing to trust Jesus to get me through this current storm, I began to look at the strength of the wind and fear for my safety. I began to sink.

I was swimming around in my circumstances again.

Ever so faithfully, and as gently as He did with Peter, Jesus reached for me in the water. He pulled me up again. He reminded me of who He is and assured me that He has the power to command the wind and seas.

Once again I started to trust. I climbed back into the boat and watched as Jesus calmed another storm.

ANGEL IN THE COFFEE SHOP

(and the angel wasn't me)

Deborah Carpenter

"**W**hy do you worry about what you will eat and what you will wear? Look at the birds of the air: they neither sow nor reap nor gather into barns, and yet your heavenly Father feeds them. Also, consider the flowers of the field. They neither toil nor spin and your Father in heaven clothes them in beauty! Are you not of more value than they? How much more does He care for you, His dear children!" (my paraphrase of Matt 6:25–34).

It was pouring rain as I left the lawyer's office. My mood was about as cheery.

I had left my husband's side at the hospital to meet with the lawyer. After the meeting, I would drive the rest of the way to my daughter's other hospital bedside where she was fighting complications from a ruptured appendix.

He sat across the big oak desk and told me the hard truth. Until there was an insurance settlement from the accident my husband had been in, our family was in dire financial trouble. That settlement could be five to ten years away. Everything we had worked towards for the last 17 years was about to amount to nothing. Bankruptcy was our only option. My only decision was whether it would be just me or both my husband and me. The hopeful solution was for just me to declare insolvency and pray that my husband would one day be able to work again to make up our losses.

He was sorry. So was I. As I drove the final miles to see my daughter I wondered how it had all come to this. It was one thing to have two loved ones in the hospital fighting for their lives. It was another thing to do it flat broke. The only money I had was two $10 bills someone had slipped me at the hospital. For coffee, they had told me. I needed that coffee now.

I pulled into the parking lot at a local coffee shop. I was soaking wet as I opened the doors and walked inside. My mind was numb. I hoped the coffee would warm my body and my heart.

I stood in the line and watched as customers waited their turn. The young lady at the till seemed to be having an issue with her order. She was dressed in black sweats and a hoodie, and both she and her clothes looked like they had seen better days. A well-dressed man and woman waited behind her, in front of me. The woman harrumphed. The man began tapping his foot and crossed his arms. The young girl looked embarrassed.

A flicker of understanding crept across my mind. Her debit card was declined. I stepped past the fancy couple and approached the girl.

"Are you having trouble with your card?"

"Yes," she replied and hurriedly finished by telling me she had thought she had enough to pay for her coffee—but she didn't.

I reached into my pocket and pulled out a $10 bill, passed it to the clerk, and told her that I would cover it. I then handed the young girl the change. "For a coffee later," I told her, and stepped back to my place in line behind the man and woman. "Have a wonderful day."

The young lady smiled, thanked me profusely and then left the coffee shop. I think she might have skipped a little.

The woman in front of me turned around and told me that it was very nice of me to do that. I just nodded and gave her half a smile. I felt a little awkward. I am sure she thought that certainly *my* debit card wouldn't be declined. But she would have been wrong.

And what had I done, really? The money wasn't even mine. The young woman and I were probably more alike than the woman in front of me thought. All I had done was see her plight. If I had seen her, it was only because God had pointed her out to me. I realized that I might not have noticed her under different circumstances. I was about to try to hold my family together with $20. She wanted a coffee and didn't have enough.

Once I got back in my car with my large coffee and cream, I sat and cried. I was humbled. I felt as though God was reminding me that He, indeed, saw me too. He would provide for my family in the same way I had just provided for the young lady—in small but miraculous ways. And He would use people just like me, who would help because He would help them see me.

I could fill pages and pages with how He provided, repeatedly. Yes, I declared bankruptcy. Yes, we lost our home. Yes, we had to start over. But no, we never went without. It didn't matter if it was school supplies for the children, gifts that first Christmas, food or clothing. We never went without, and I never went without a cup of coffee.

I am still humbled when I recall that day and the days that followed. That was the day I met an angel dressed in black. God sent her to me so that I would see in real life what He was doing and was going to do for my family. It was the day He showed me that He saw me and that He cared for me. And by doing so, He opened my eyes to all the ways I could respond to Him with an open hand and a willing heart. Whenever I think of her, I remind myself to keep my eyes open to see what God is going to do.

In truth, I became rich that day. No matter what the lawyer said.

MOUNTAINTOPS AND VALLEYS

Kerry Robideau

"Winter is over; the winter rains are over, gone! Spring flowers are in blossom all over" (Song of Songs 2:11, MSG).

My husband and I love to be in the Rocky Mountains of southern Alberta. We love the majesty of them and wonder about the mystery of their formation. As we prepare to hike, however, we also prepare for the quick change in weather that may happen. There can be sunshine one moment in the mountains and rain or snow the next.

There is a hike we like to do that takes us up above the treeline to a beautiful glacier. I always look forward to seeing the flora, and taking pictures along the way. My husband and kids always bring garbage bags to use as crazy carpets and slide down the snowy embankment tucked beside the glacier. A cool treat in the middle of a hot summer.

The tops of mountains represent many things to me. They represent the ability to see above my circumstances, or the ability to enjoy the beauty of my surroundings. What makes a long hike even more meaningful is the realization after a hard journey that it was worth the struggle to get there. The mountains also allow me to wonder, to rest, and to enjoy.

All of these aspects are significant to me as I ponder the last few years compared to where I am today. I have walked through circumstances that felt at times like "the valley of the shadow of death" (Ps

23)—a dark, dry place of turbulence and tribulations. Outward circumstances brought inward suffering, a war within my own heart and mind. That season of winter lasted several long years, and I often wondered if, let alone when, it would ever change.

Then it began to happen. Little glimpses of hope and life appeared. God set up divine appointments, opened up doors of opportunity to walk into freedom, spoke to me of His love, and helped me set my eyes back on Him even though my circumstances hadn't changed drastically. Winter began to turn to spring.

Now, as I sit on this mountain and look back on the path I travelled in the valley, I see more clearly how God changed me through that whole journey. God is more interested in freeing me from *me* than He is in freeing me from my outward condition. I am reminded that I was bought with a price; I am not my own (1 Cor 6:20). Jesus has His perfect timing even when I feel confused and hurt, not understanding at the time why He allows the suffering. He is still good even when He says "Wait" or "No." Suffering brings character growth, realization of who I am, and deeper intimacy with Christ.

However, the path to get to that point wasn't easy. It took all my will to keep going at times and I struggled with despair, depression, and fear. It took tears, courage, tears, prayer (in tears), 'shoulder to shoulder' friends, shifting my eyes off myself and onto God, and an open heart to His potential and what He wanted to do. It took humility and the submission of my will to His. My heart was broken, then melted and reshaped to fit the image He had for me. It took the valley experience to make much of this happen.

The Song of Songs is a picture to me of the depth of God's love for each of us. He cherishes us to a depth our hearts and minds are too finite to comprehend. That's why He gave us so many images of His love in Scripture. He wants the winter season of our souls to shape us but He also wants the season to end. He longs to give us the growth and newness of life that spring has to offer.

I may be on a mountaintop right now, but I am not meant to stay there forever. At some point I have to get off the top and head back into the valley. There I will learn and grow some more.

Whether you are halfway up the mountain, at the top, or still travelling through the valley, take hope. God will see you through. Will you partner with Him on your journey to make change happen?

"It is not the mountain we conquer but ourselves." — Edmund Hillary, first man to summit Mt. Everest, accompanied by his Sherpa, Tenzing Norgay

HEALING WOUNDS

Connie Lucille Peachey

What does it look like to allow God's love to touch our wounds?

I woke up in the middle of the night with my knee throbbing. It felt like it was going to explode. With every beat of my heart I could feel the pain—the worst pain I had ever had. I was in grade 5.

A few weeks earlier, my brother and I had been biking to school. I had only looked away briefly, but in a split second his bike was in my path and my front tire hooked his back tire, causing me to go sprawling along the gravel road. My knee was ripped open and bleeding. We hopped back on our bikes and continued on to school, blood coursing down my leg. At school my teacher bandaged my knee and we continued on with the day like nothing had happened. At home my mom fixed it up a little better, making sure it was good and clean.

A few weeks later, with my knee scabbed over and nicely healing, I was on a skateboard flying through the cul-de-sac when I hit some gravel. Once again I found myself sliding along the ground as the pavement and gravel tore like sandpaper through my already-wounded knee. Now it was really ripped open. I fixed it up as best I could and, because I am no sissy, got right back to playing. It did not take long, however, for infection to take hold and now, in the middle of the night, I could no longer stand the pain.

My mom took one look at my knee and knew just what to do. We lived out in the country, and back then one did not just set off to the doctor for every bump and scrape. So she boiled some water, then added a bit of baking soda and some salt. With the water as hot as possible short of burning my flesh, she dipped a clean cloth into it and began cleaning my wound, removing the pus, the gravel, and the infection. I was not a fan of this type of pain. She was firm that I needed to sit still and allow her to do her job if I wanted my knee to heal properly. I had to give her access and allow her to touch the part that hurt so badly, the torn skin and flesh. Wow, that hurt!

I still have an angry purple scar on my knee from those accidents, but underneath it has healed beautifully and I now no longer have pain at the injury site. I have not forgotten the injury, but the pain has been healed.

What about soul pain? What about the wounds you have sustained to your mind, your will, your emotions? What about your broken heart? The pain may have been inflicted when you were a child, or perhaps it happened yesterday. "Forgive and forget" is a mantra that perhaps needs to be dismantled. As Christians it is easy to say, "Oh, that is under the blood of Jesus. I have forgiven them." While forgiveness is necessary, it is also necessary to get the gravel out of the wound before it can heal. Just putting a bandage on it will not address the infection. Remember what happened. Call it what it is. Feel the pain. Invite Jesus into the memory. Ask Him to show you where He was when it all happened. Give Him permission to reach in and touch the wound and bring His healing to you. He understands pain and suffering.

"Surely he took up our infirmities and carried our sorrows, yet we considered him stricken by God, smitten by him, and afflicted. But he was pierced for our transgressions, he was crushed for our iniquities; the punishment that brought us peace was upon him, and by his wounds we are healed" (Isa 53:4–5).

Covering up and hiding that which has brought us pain will not result in healing. Revisiting the pain may seem like too big a risk. Who wants to feel that again? Self-medicating with drugs and/or pleasure in order to mask our pain has become an epidemic in our country. Until we bring our pain to Jesus for healing it will not go away. The effects of our injury will surface again in some place in our lives.

"Praise be to the God and Father of our Lord Jesus Christ, the Father of compassion and the God of all comfort, who comforts us in all our troubles, so that we can comfort those in any trouble with the comfort we ourselves have received from God" (2 Cor 1:3–4).

Jesus will not force you to bring your pain to Him for healing. But He is also kind and compassionate. He is totally trustworthy and will handle your pain with care. He is familiar with pain and suffering and knows just what is needed to bring healing to your soul. I invite you to bring Him your broken heart and wounded soul. Only Jesus heals, and heal He does!

REST AND REFLECTION

Your Name

Where is one area of your life that you feel God may be able to use your story to encourage others?

What is a practical step that you could take to share your story?

SWIRLING SNOWFLAKES

Lynda Blazina

I was on my way to work as the huge, fluffy snowflakes started falling. With them came familiar feelings of dread—dread of the cold, the lack of light, the need for bulky winter clothes... Did I mention the *cold*!

Feelings of frustration also surfaced, as this was only the first week in September. September! It seemed that June had just passed and here we were, at the end of summer. Even at the end of summer, we should have had another whole season to enjoy before winter hit. It shouldn't be snowing yet! I was not in any way ready for winter.

The snow fell harder and thicker the further I drove. I was a little early for work, so I pulled over at one point and looked up. The snow was coming down in great big clumps of flakes, some of them the size of apples. Softly landing on the earth, they were quickly accumulating and forming a white blanket on the green grass, the coloured leaves, and the peaks of houses.

It took my breath away. It was incredibly gorgeous!

In that moment, suddenly and unexpectedly, the Lord did a work in my heart. How often had I lost out on moments of wonder and beauty because I was stuck in the dread of the season? How often had my thoughts, consumed by circumstances, kept my eyes from seeing glimmering moments of God's grace and truth?

I also realized that even though this moisture was fluffy, it was much needed for our dry earth. God was providing what was needed, even though it wasn't through my preferred method!

God was showing me that there are moments of beauty to be savoured even in the midst of seasons that are less than enjoyable. I didn't need to be so immersed in dread that I couldn't see the beauty of swirling flakes floating and dancing their way to the ground.

He was also showing me that He provides in His time and in His way. I need to trust in His provision, even when it looks different than the way I've envisioned it.

I took a deep breath and made the decision to enjoy this temporary wonderland. I would enjoy the sparkle and cleanness of the white, realizing again that it was actually just the end of summer. Because of that fact, within a couple of days, the white would probably all be melted into the continued colour of fall.

I asked the Lord in that moment to prepare my heart for wonder in the midst of hard circumstances. Winter is inevitable, but I want to watch with anticipation, looking for the beauty and provision that God will bring in any and every season.

"The rain and snow come down from the heavens and stay on the ground to water the earth. They cause the grain to grow, producing seed for the farmer and bread for the hungry" (Isa 55:10).

WHERE IS MY IDENTITY?

Lisa Clarke

I sat at the table in our home, trying to take everything in. It was a cool Friday evening, and I had just put a warm, steaming supper on the table. For a moment my mind slipped back to a time when my oldest daughter was freely reciting Psalm 100. Then another memory flashed through my mind of her attempts to memorize Philippians 4:8–9:

"Finally, brothers and sisters, whatever is true, whatever is noble, whatever is right, whatever is pure, whatever is lovely, whatever is admirable—if anything is excellent or praiseworthy—think about such things… And the God of peace will be with you." This was one of her favourite passages.

Then she said it, the words that I somehow had feared, "I'm gay."

At that moment, I felt a flood of love. The words she had just spoken didn't hold the same power over me as I had once thought they would. I didn't fall apart or say anything really stupid. I just sat weeping slightly. I told her I loved her. I must admit that my weeping was mixed with mourning. I knew change was coming, and that her boyfriend of three years would no longer be a part of our lives in the same way. The idea of accepting and welcoming him into our family was dying in front of me. I was having to let go of things that would never be.

As I went up to bed that night, I lifted her up to God. My mind flashed to my earlier years, before I knew Jesus. I had looked for human love to define me and give me identity. I sought out many men during those years to fill the void, which brought me false security. Even though I couldn't exactly relate to what my daughter had shared, I could understand the emptiness and the void in her life. I too had hoped that I would find love to satisfy my deep longing to belong and be accepted.

What I didn't know then, but am starting to understand now, is that the more God pursues and draws us into relationship with Him, the more we begin to understand our identity. Our true identity is found in Christ. When we lose sight of that, we lose our compass and the world tells us that anything goes. I think we often experience conflict because our faith and the world we are in collide. We have to make tough decisions and even tougher choices. Several Scriptures help guide my understanding of identity:

"For in Christ all the fullness of Deity lives in bodily form, and in Christ you have been brought to fullness. He is the head over every power and authority" (Col 2:9–10).

"But whoever is united with the Lord is one with him in spirit" (1 Cor 6:17).

"Now you are the body of Christ, and each one of you is part of it" (1 Cor 12:27).

Finally, 1 Pet 2:9 gives this deep statement of our identity:

"But you are a chosen people, a royal priesthood, a holy nation, God's special possession, that you may declare the praises of Him who called you out of darkness into His wonderful light."

There are many other passages that go even further to explain where we should find identity, but these suffice to give us much to ponder and reflect on. Join me in praying that the people we love might find their identity in the one who created us, who knows us, and who loves us—the one who is also the King of kings and Lord of lords. Jesus the King is God incarnate, who unites us to Himself and calls us the Body of Christ, chosen, holy, special, and His possession.

A TIME FOR WEEPING

Charleen Raschke

"A time to weep and a time to laugh, a time to mourn and a time to dance" (Eccles 3:4).

I recently found myself strolling through a large department store. I headed to the baby area. My young friend was nearing her due date and I wanted to be prepared with a gift to take to the hospital. She knew she was having a baby girl, so I was scouting out girly things.

As happy as I was for her, shopping for her baby came with a sting. It had only been a couple of months since our loss.

My hand gently stroked the material of baby blankets, newborn dresses and outfits. They were soft to the touch and I imagined our little granddaughter. I should have been shopping for her!

Our tiny little grandbaby was still growing inside her momma when we lost her. "Silently born" was typed on her death certificate. I never had the chance to meet this precious little girl before she was ushered into the very presence of Jesus.

Waves of grief come and they go. They hit with no warning at all.

My very pregnant friend will meet her daughter any day now. I've been asked to be on call in case her husband is working when she goes into labour. I am honoured to be given this role, truly honoured! However, there is a cost that comes with being in such close proximity to my friend's utter joy and happiness. It magnifies my own loss as a Nana.

I will embrace this incredibly special time of welcoming my friend's little one into her family, and I will continue to choke back tears and have moments of biting my lip, attempting to keep my emotions at bay. Just the other day, I invited the grief in and allowed myself to feel our little girl's absence and loss once again. Hot tears streamed down my face for a good part of the day. She was remembered and acknowledged as she should be.

When the time comes for me to hold and cuddle my friend's new baby girl, my little granddaughter will be very close to my heart. My arms will feel the ache of being empty of her.

My faith in Jesus comforts my heart. I know without a doubt I will meet our little one someday. I know she is okay. Her spirit is very much alive.

I sometimes imagine her running and jumping for joy, just as she was when technicians would try to capture her picture for her ultrasounds. One day, she will be showing me around heaven and all she will have discovered before I join her there. She'll be able to tell me of when she heard her mom's and dad's and big brother's voices echoing from the womb. She knows she is loved.

Because of Jesus, I have so much to look forward to! I have so much hope for the future, when my granddaughter and her Nana will finally get to laugh and dance together.

TRUST IN HIM

Connie Lucille Peachey

"Then Jesus said, 'Come to me, all of you who are weary and carry heavy burdens, and I will give you rest. Take my yoke upon you. Let me teach you, because I am humble and gentle at heart, and you will find rest for your souls. For my yoke is easy to bear, and the burden I give you is light'" (Matt 11:28–30, NLT).

"It's okay to not be okay."

How many of you have heard this mantra? How many have adopted it as truth? I see it as partly true, but also partly as an insidious lie from the enemy of our souls to keep us in bondage. It is okay to *admit* we are not okay. In fact, that is the beginning of self-awareness which is necessary if we are to grow in our relationship with Jesus. We cannot admit something we are not aware of. And we will not confess and repent for things we do not realize we are guilty of. However, could it be that when we embrace "It's okay to not be okay" and are content to live there, we are excusing ourselves from having to move forward? Could this then leave us with little or no motivation to grow?

I feel that it is *not* okay to operate long in the state of 'not okay.' God does not want it. He does not design it. He loves us too much to allow us to live 'not okay.' He certainly allows us to be in process, and to take an occasional hiatus for rest. But He is not okay with *leaving us* 'not okay.' Having said that, I don't believe He wants us to 'pull ourselves up by our bootstraps' and *pretend* we are okay either.

Nov 20, 2017 – Journal entry in response to this thinking:

God, You gave me a long season to grieve, to mourn, to rest in 'hospital.' But You never abandoned me on my heap of ashes. You were always right there bringing comfort and healing, while soothing and dressing my wounds. You gifted me with time to heal, but You were not okay with my pain and sorrow. Thank You for Your love. Thank You for ever inviting me into Your presence. Thank You for healing my broken heart. Thank You that Your goal is always to be in a growing relationship with me—always moving me forward. Even in my season in the deep dark valley, we always keep moving; always communicating. Yes, we stop to rest as needed. It's a beautiful rhythm of rest, learn, yoke (suggests forward motion as it is used for work), rest, peace.

At times God sets us apart. Not so we 'slough off' but so He can do the hard work of inner transformation in our souls without distractions. The passage from Matthew quoted above gives us a glimpse into the heart of the Father. When we are not okay, He says, "Come to Me. Rest in Me. Take My yoke, it's not nearly as heavy as the one you are trying to carry. Now let's do this together. Learn from Me along the way. You'll find that I care, that I am a gentleman, and what I ask you to carry is far lighter than you can imagine." His exhortations in this passage give us reason to believe He is not okay with us remaining 'not okay.' And yet, twice He mentions *rest*. Rest from striving to 'keep it together,' and 'rest for your souls' (mind, will, emotions). Inner peace.

I spent months grieving a myriad of traumatic losses. Looking on from the outside, it might have appeared that I was stuck in the place of 'not being okay.' It's true that I laid aside the burden that was too heavy for me to bear. I rested with Jesus and allowed Him to minister to my broken heart. But I did not stay there. God is ever moving me toward healing. Much inner healing happened before it began to show on the outside. More healing is on the way. God is okay with me being in process, but He is not okay with leaving me bleeding all over the place. He is not in a rush and He is not nervous that this 'healing thing' is taking so long.

God's yoke truly is easy and the burden He asks me to carry is light. It's when I try to carry more than what is mine to carry that things get heavy and I find myself once again in a state of 'not okay.' Then I remember the rhythm He invites me to: "Come to Me. Rest in Me. Take My yoke. Learn from Me. Rest your souls." Shalom... all is well.

I invite you to examine whether "It's okay to not be okay" is just a passing season, or whether it has become a place where you live. I invite you to respond to Christ's invitation to come, learn, rest, and trade your yoke for His. I invite you to trust Him to bring health to your soul today; to trust Him to move you ever gently forward out of the season of 'not okay.' He loves you too much to leave you there.

SHAME OFF YOU

Charleen Raschke

Shame. What is it? According to Dictionary.com, it is: "the painful feeling arising from the consciousness of something dishonorable, improper, ridiculous, etc., done by oneself or another" (Nov 2018).

I don't know about you, but I think a lot of us grew up hearing something like this, "Shame on you!" I can still picture a finger pointing my way and shaking as I heard that phrase.

Shame is not the same as guilt. According to therapist Dr. Sandra D. Wilson, "Guilt tells me I made a mistake. Shame shouts that I am a mistake" (*Released from Shame*, 2002).

While we certainly should feel guilt when we do something wrong, shame is a whole other thing. The heart of God actually says, "Shame *off* you!" He longs to remove our shame, regardless of whether it is shame we placed on ourselves because of our own actions, or shame placed on us by someone else.

I have experienced both. Most of us have.

As a very young child, for example, I felt shame on me that was so heavy, and there for so long, that it felt very 'normal' to me. And yet, I was innocent; I did nothing to 'deserve' it. In my broken childhood, the sexual abuse I experienced made me feel as though I did something wrong. I was being held captive in an emotional prison.

As an older child and teen, I experienced more shame—like a draped, heavy, dirty blanket, flung over my shoulders. It weighed me down, accused me and held me captive for many, many years. Some of this was because of my own poor choices, but much of it was directly connected to my sexual abuse.

When you live in that sort of prison for a very long time, you don't really know there is anything better for you. The darkness has been with you for so long that it 'feels' very normal for you.

Because of the shame I carried, I didn't think I was actually worthy of love and I didn't really know how to receive love. Shame had been with me for so long that it became a part of who I thought I was. Entangled in my heart, like a filter that would stop real love from going any deeper. If you can't receive love, you can't truly give it either. Shame was affecting everything.

I was starving. Starving for real love. Starving for real identity. This led to a heart that was shrivelled and dry.

I had no idea freedom awaited me. I had no idea that Jesus held freedom out for me to access. It wasn't until several years later, through the gentleness of a godly counsellor, that Jesus began to unravel the threads of my brokenness. He began to shine His glorious light on the truth of my abuse and my shame, and began to show me a beautiful exchange. A better way to a free and whole life. Paid for in full on the cross.

"You, LORD, are my lamp; the LORD turns my darkness into light" (2 Sam 22:29). His light exposes lies and He can turn shame into hope.

After my counsellor began to help me to gain a new perspective, I began to allow the light of Jesus to dispel the dark places in my heart where lies were believed and embraced. I entered a new season with God.

As my heart was being healed, God caused a hunger for good things in the deeper parts of me. As I walked into healing and hunger, my identity began to change. My identity as His Beloved began to grow as healthy roots were being nourished.

I was learning how to Be-loved. And what a difference His love makes!

"Those who look to Him are radiant; their faces are never covered with shame" (Ps 34:5). As I looked to Him, my shame couldn't stay. As I looked to Him, my identity was rewired to His truth about who He is and about who I am created to be in Him.

— DAY 90 —

SPRING IS COMING

Lynda Blazina

"Let us acknowledge the LORD; let us press on to acknowledge him. As surely as the sun rises, he will appear; he will come to us like the winter rains, like the spring rains that water the earth" (Hosea 6:3).

As I sat in church with two of my three children, I fought off the tears. If you had been able to put on a pair of spiritual lenses, you would have seen that all three of us were bloodied and scarred from the past year. Tired and worn from months of intense spiritual, emotional, and even physical battles.

Icy winds from a long spiritual winter had taken their toll.

But in this place where the Lord had directed our footsteps to fall, there was sudden warmth blowing through my life. As their pastor spoke each Sunday, I felt as if the Holy Spirit had given him the words to speak directly to me and my kids. Words of strength and healing. Words of hope and power. Words that brought tears of deeply-seeded joy.

The ice was starting to melt.

As we dove into Scripture each week, and the words came alive to me in a way that they hadn't for a very long time, I began to hear from God again. I began to see things that had been buried beneath months' and years' worth of spiritual snowdrifts. Even though there were still plenty of piles of snow around, I began to see little blades of green growth poking up here and there.

I could sense a shift happening in my soul. The 'nights' didn't seem so long. Things had started to awaken.

As well as attending church with my kids, I had an amazing group of women who were surrounding me with their love and support. They showed no judgement or criticism toward my chaos and brokenness. They loved me and allowed me to grieve in their presence. They encouraged me to seek the Lord for healing. They spent hours praying for me.

Little buds started appearing on the trees, still fragile in their jackets and vulnerable to the cold.

God again began to direct my steps. I began to take a course on healing through discipleship. Through this course, it seemed my steps were taking me through the mud and puddles that were forming as things thawed. Even though this indication of spring was messy, it meant that the season was continuing to change.

My husband and a couple of close friends were sources of winter and spring rains. Whenever I needed them, whenever I reached out, they were there. With no demands that I defend my quietness, or sometimes even withdrawal, they supported me in love and compassion.

Each of these people, each of these spaces that God carved out for me, were His loving design for the change of seasons. There were times when I felt the need to "press on to acknowledge Him." Times when joy and life didn't come easily or naturally. But I have yet to spend a year where the only season is winter. Sometimes the wait for warmth seems long and tedious, sometimes a spring storm will blow through, but if you are in a place of feeling the effects of winter, hold on. Start looking for signs of spring. Revel in even the minute indications that we worship the God who changes the seasons and will bring you into spring.

No matter how long the winter is … spring is coming!

ACKNOWLEDGEMENTS

First and foremost, all thanks and praise go to Jesus, for working in our lives in every way to bring this book to fruition. Because of Him, our stories are being redeemed and used for His glory.

Brenda would like to dedicate her writings to her sons Josiah, Jacob and John (Alec) along with the multitude of family and friends who have been a constant source of encouragement in her life.

Charleen would like to thank her husband John, her children, Micah, Stefanie and Dylan. Her parents and her incredibly encouraging friends, Bonnie Lee (sister), Kerry Robideau, Lynda Blazina, Norlyn Tangjerd and Tangie Shields for believing in this and other writing projects she has stepped into. Each one is a part of the cheering squad!

Connie would like to thank her husband Tom for all the meals cooked and dishes washed allowing her to bury herself in writing. And a special thank you to her mom (Betty Siemens Martens) for the word pictures she painted as Connie practised countless hours at the piano, training her mind to look for creative imagery in the simple things of life.

Deborah owes a debt of gratitude to her husband Andrew, her children Rebekkah, Sarah, Joshua, Caleb and Grace, and friends too numerous to name here, for their belief in her even when she did not believe.

Kerry would like to thank her husband Larry for his support and for being her chief editor. She would like to thank her cheerleading squad: Kim, Norlyn, Charleen, Heidi, Josh, Jane, Bev. They have all been an amazing prayer support and encouragement to her, each in their own way. Also thank you to Shannon for believing in life beyond work and the encouragement to keep writing.

Lisa: I would like to thank my husband Bryan and our daughters Jessica and Bryanna for their support through this writing project. I dedicate these words I have penned in memory of my daughter Melissa. I am thankful for the encouragement of my friend Leanne Cripps and one of my mentors Lorraine DeBruyn. I also appreciate the prayers and support of my parents. Lastly, I acknowledge Lynda Blazina who gave this opportunity and encouraged me when I didn't think I could do it.

Lynda would like to thank her husband Max, her kids Ryshon, Christian and Tryse, and her friends Mary-Joan Heide, Vonne Lewis, Abbie Macdonald, Kim Pangracs and Kathy Morales for believing this project could actually happen and fanning her dream into flame.

Ryshon would like to thank her mom for forcing her to write. But the book turned out great so it's all good! She would also like to thank Taylor, Kieran, Bailea and Candra for encouraging her in all of her crazy endeavours.

Stefanie would like to thank her mom first and foremost for encouraging her along the way and believing in her as a writer. Also her husband Drew and two daughters for being the best cheerleaders. Finally, her dad and her dearest friends Kayle, Amy, Jacqueline and Amory for being her constants and always believing in her.

All devotionals were edited by Alicia Hein and Elaine Phillips. Thank you for making our words sound the best they could, in order for our stories to be communicated with clarity. We love you both and value you as part of our team.

ENDORSEMENTS

It has been my greatest pleasure to preview the devotional *Journey Through Winter*. Wouldn't it be wonderful if life could always be lived in the sunshine, warmth, love, joy, and happiness of the summer season?! Our Father in heaven, however, never guaranteed us a trouble-free life. In fact, we all know that the summers of our lives can quickly be replaced by seasons of difficulty, seasons of seemingly never-ending winters, loneliness, sadness, and frustrations.

These winter seasons can challenge our faith, cripple us emotionally and leave us feeling deserted. The fact is, it's easy to be a good person, wife, husband, sister, brother, friend, Christian, when our lives are going well. The real test of our faith and our character happens when life goes sideways on us. When we face adversity, we often begin doubting God—which is exactly what the Devil would have us do! Satan has done his job if he can make us feel distant from God and doubting the Lord's purpose for our lives.

Having endured my share of winter seasons, including the loss of my first wife Darlene to cancer, the death of my sister, and many other life challenges, I have struggled through the winters of my life. I wish that I had been able to draw on the many encouraging words and Scriptures that are found in *Journey Through Winter*. I believe the Scriptures and perspectives of the authors would have strengthened me and hurried my journey back into a more abundant life and relationship with Christ. Everyone needs inspiration when times are difficult and that is exactly what can be found in this devotional.

One of my favourite Scriptures reads as follows: "Small is the gate and narrow the road that leads to life, and only a few find it" (Matt 7:14). If you are journeying through a difficult season in your life, or if you know of someone in your circle of influence who is, the devotional *Journey Through Winter* is a daily must-read! The words contained in it whisper God's soothing words into your heart and soul, encouraging you through the gate and down the road of life, helping you through the winter seasons of your life.

For every winter season we face I believe God has sunshine and warmth planned for us as our reward. I believe *Journey Through Winter* will help you move to a new summer season in your lives in a better fashion than if you simply try to do it on your own. That is my prayer for you. God bless.

—**Tom Watson**, Life and Business Coach, international award-winning personality, speaker, consultant, bestselling author of *Man Shoes*

Journey Through Winter will certainly shatter any mistaken ideas that following Jesus comes with built-in immunity against the storms of life. But these authentic—even raw—devotional readings also reveal that a walk through fire can result in a faith of tempered steel. Listen in as these women courageously share how they have leaned hard on Jesus and His Word and found that He is faithful. No doubt, their stories will challenge and strengthen your own faith. Intriguingly, they've even carved out space for you to journal a few of your own stories of God's faithfulness in a season of winter.

—**Dr. Susan Booth**, **PhD**, Professor of Evangelism and Missions at Canadian Southern Baptist Seminary and College, author of *Longing for Home*

It is impossible to go through this life without encountering seasons in which we feel lost and alone. In these seasons the temptation is often to pull back and withdraw even further, but you don't need to do that. You don't need to hide or put on a mask. God the Father invites you to pour your heart out to Him.

In *Journey Through Winter*, the authors invite you to journey with them as they share personal stories and testimonies of going through hard times. With more than one writer, they offer more than one voice, more than one story. Which means, absolutely everyone reading the words within these pages will find something that will resonate with them, some form of hope and encouragement.

Don't attempt to go it alone. Take the hands they are extending and walk with them through all seasons of life.

—**Lori Heitrich,** Grief Recovery Specialist, author of *Losing Lance: One Life Matters*

Journey Through Winter inspires and comforts readers with truth from God's Word. Through personal experiences of adversity, disappointment and pain, these women share honestly about inviting God into brokenness. This book is filled with beautiful stories of God giving hope and healing deep wounds. Reading the devotions will leave you feeling like you have had a cup of coffee and a conversation with a compassionate, encouraging friend who has been there.

—**Kathy Morales**, National Team Leader for CNBC Women, Canadian National Baptist Convention

How do we navigate through the tough seasons in our lives? *Journey Through Winter* is written by some very remarkable women who have braved and weathered the storms of life by relying fully on God, and finding comfort and strength in His Word. If winter has you in its icy grip, prepare yourself for a satisfying thaw as you read through this collection of devotions and personal testimonies that will warm you through and through.

—**Lynn Dove**, author of the *Wounded Trilogy* and Canadian Christian Writing award-winner for her blog: *Journey Thoughts* (lynndove.com)

Life is painful, but God is good, and present, and loving. The authors of *Journey Through Winter* share how God has met them in the midst of some of the hard realities of life—rape, ministry challenges, living with disabilities, abuse, and divorce, to name a few. These devotionals offer hope, perspective, and a warm hug. Listen in, and learn.

—**Ruth L. Snyder**, author of *Equipped: Ephesians 6 Devotionals to Empower and Make You Victorious in Everyday Struggles*

If you've ever wondered where you fit in God's story, this book is for you. The devotions in these pages are a powerful testament to the presence of God no matter your own life story or situation. These women will invite you into their lives and you will find yourself changed in the process. You will find a place here, and in the midst of their pain and suffering, you will find yourself on these pages. Come and connect here and God will speak to you in ways you least expect it.

—**Kim Pangracs**, MSW

Journey Through Winter rocks! It's raw, real and refreshing. I love these gutsy women being truly authentic against the façade of the current social-media backdrop. No fluff here. No pretence. No makeup. Just honest, heart-wrenching stories that often mirror our sometimes-confusing hurtful reality, but unmistakably reveal a message of hope.

The book couldn't be any more God-drenched. Each difficult story of trials and pain of a wisely–faced winter's cold helps the reader find shelter in the promises and presence of God.

"My heart is in anguish within me; I would hurry to my place of shelter, far from the tempest and storm" (Ps 55:4, 8).

Get this book done! I have a list of hurting women in my world that could use a copy.

—**Dr. Dave Currie**, speaker, author, therapist
President of Doing Family Right
(DoingFamilyRight.com)